THE GRANITE MILE

A farewell to trams. *Little time was lost between the incineration of the last of Aberdeen's tram fleet at the Beach in May 1958 and the lifting of the rails in Union Street.*
West of the Music Hall, the YMCA building and the Royal Northern Club (Crimonmogate's House) are still in existence.

Looking from Holburn Junction east to the Castlegate on a sunny Saturday in 1962. Buses rule!

THE GRANITE MILE

The Story of Aberdeen's Union Street

Diane Morgan

BLACK & WHITE PUBLISHING

First published in 2008
This edition first published in 2010
by Black & White Publishing Ltd
29 Ocean Drive, Edinburgh, EH6 6JL

1 3 5 7 9 10 8 6 4 2   10 11 12 13 14

ISBN: 978 1 84502 326 3

A CIP Catalogue record for this book is available from the British Library.

The photographs drawn from *The Aberdeen Journal's* archives can be purchased from the Photosales Department.
Tel. 01224 338011, or by visiting
www.ajlphotosales.co.uk

Typeset by
Creative Link

Printed and bound in China by
Printplus Ltd

ACKNOWLEDGEMENTS

I am much indebted, for help and advice received, to Pat Sutherland, Frank Donnelly, Michael Thomson, Forbes McCallum, Norman Mackenzie, Innes MacLeod, Guy Bentinck, Irene Bryce, John Michie, Connie Leith, Alison Cameron, Willie Anderson, Anne Simpson and Alex Mitchell; and to Duncan Smith and Robert Stewart of Aberdeen Journals Library. I owe a particular debt of gratitude to Susan McKay, Retail Manager, Thom Cooper, Photosales Manager and Lee Corpe, photographer.

The photographs published in *The Granite Mile* came from the files of *Aberdeen Journals* except as noted below:

The Author's Collection pages xvi, 6, 15, 16, 20, 33, 46, 73, 75, 76 (top), 93 (bottom), 113, 121, 122, 131, 144, 164, 166 (lower), 168, 178, 179 and all advertisements.

I have pleasure in acknowledging permission to reproduce copyright images provided by the following:

Aberdeen Art Gallery & Museums Collections page 72
Michie, Chemists page 123
Stewart Milne Developments page 140
The Royal Commission on the Ancient and Historic Monuments of Scotland pages 60 (right), 66(top left), 136
Kitty Strachan pages 142-3
The George Washington Wilson Collection/University of Aberdeen page 66 (top right)
Martin Watt pages 88-9
Winrams Bookshop pages 84, 148, 174

The illustrations on pages 30, 163 are by J A Sutherland

The photographs drawn from *Aberdeen Journals'* archives can be purchased from the Photosales Department: telephone 01224 338011 or visit www.ajlphotosales.co.uk

BY THE SAME AUTHOR

Lost Aberdeen
Lost Aberdeen: The Outskirts
Lost Aberdeen: The Freedom Lands
Footdee and her Shipyards
Round About Mounthooly
The Spital
The Spital Lands
Old Aberdeen
A Monumental Business: The Story of A & J Robertson (Granite) Ltd 1876-2001

The Royal Bank
of Scotland at No
78 Union Street.

Contents

*A **once familiar row** of shops below the Gloucester Hotel.*

Union Terrace Gardens, *looking south, on a lazy summer's day in 1964. The large building, top, was C&As, now a Travelodge.*

PREFACE

In Chapter Four of *The Granite Mile*, reference was made to the persistence over the years of schemes to reinstate Union Terrace Gardens which lie below Union Bridge and Union Terrace. A grander style was demanded, more in keeping with its position in the heart of the city. Such schemes have faded away owning to lack of funding, downright unpopularity, or both. The latest scheme made its appearance as *The Granite Mile* was going to press towards the end of 2008, providing no opportunity to report on its progress. 'An ill-considered proposal' commented Norman Marr, architect and former town planner. It was tantamount to the destruction of the Gardens, and has left many Aberdonians shaken, stirred and even shattered. This section of the Introduction brings that part of our story up to date.

The opening section of *The Granite Mile* describes a historic moment in July 1801 when the foundation stone of the new bridge over the Denburn was laid. This, the future Union Bridge, would link both sides of the Denburn Valley, the ravine which for centuries had barred the city's expansion. The newly baptised Union Street – 'the Union Street Viaduct' as it was called at this juncture – was creeping up from the Castlegate. When the Bridge was eventually completed it carried Union Street over the Valley to the spacious plain beckoning beyond. Here New Aberdeen, the handsome granite west end of the city came into being.

At the time of the foundation ceremony, the floor of the northwest side of the Valley was a common bleachgreen. In earlier times a doocot had stood on the slopes above, shown on Parson Gordon's Plan of 1666, hence Doocot Brae and the area around, the Corbie Heugh, was the nesting place of many a crow down the years. In the nineteenth century the rather scrubby Heugh was transformed by the brilliant work of two architects. James Matthews created 'a pleasure park for the people' from what had been, at the north end at least, largely slum property. Alexander Marshall Mackenzie elegantly redesigned the Heugh to co-ordinate with Union Terrace and Union Bridge and so created Union Terrace Gardens. They remain, not only a surviving fragment of the original level of the town, but they mark the place where the new city soared above the medieval town, a memorable part of Aberdeen's heritage.

The Gardens whose natural hollow offered shelter from chilly winds became a welcome haven of greenery, enhanced by tiers of terracing. Owned by the City Council, it remained a pleasure park until well into the post-war period with pipe bands, open air draughts and dancing, with bedding plants laid out in rich heraldic display in season. City centre workers enjoyed *al fresco* lunches in the summer time and latterly, in the winter, there was an ice rink. Unfortunately, by the early 1980s, perhaps earlier, when the drug scene arrived in Aberdeen, the Gardens became a 'no go' area for many. Their arches which run under Union Terrace – the old Bow Brig is still down there – had become a haunt of drunks and drug addicts. Successive city councils turned a blind eye. The handsome Victorian toilets, one of the Gardens' gems, were crassly repaired when necessary, then closed down altogether to keep the druggies out.

With its prime position, the Gardens were a unique natural feature that many other cities would be delighted to possess. Their deterioration could have been remedied by a police presence and the crowds lured back by a resumption of activities, an attractive planting programme and last but not least the reinstatement and 'manning' of the Victorian toilets. This initiative was never taken, but there were crumbs of comfort in that the whole length of the Gardens, always neatly maintained, could still be enjoyed from the north side of Union Bridge, with the splendid granite panorama of Education (the Public Library), Salvation (St Mark's Church) and Damnation (His Majesty's Theatre) on Rosemount Viaduct beyond.

By 2008 a new plan had emerged, from Peacock Visual Arts, formerly Peacock Printmakers who were given permission to build a new centre near the old 'Doocot' Brae. Their architect's plans revealed a series of undulating grass-like roofs embedded in the western slopes, resembling the hillside fortress of some early central Asian tribe. This was not to everyone's taste, and moreover, a sizeable number of Aberdonians are purists, conceding that the Gardens need to be upgraded, and made more accessible but otherwise should be left in peace. But with 75% of funding required for that project secured, a sigh of relief went up. At least the remaining acres would remain safe from further tampering. Above all, the magnificent view across Rosemount Viaduct would remain intact. They had reckoned without the proposals of a local oil tycoon, Sir Ian Wood and his associates, who launched a far-reaching scheme on an unsuspecting public in November 2008. Little else has been spoken about in the city since then, and the Peacock plans have apparently been blown out of the water.

Sir Ian had offered £50 million of his personal fortune to replace Union Terrace Gardens with a City Square, whose creation would ensure the economic future of the city. This, the City Square Project required the Gardens to be completely dug out and replaced with a subterranean steel and concrete structure comprising several levels and topped off with a concrete 'lid' – the Square itself, extending above ground to five acres to cover the railway line and the dual carriageway on the east side of the Denburn Valley. Level access to the Square would be provided from Union Bridge, Union Terrace, the Denburn Viaduct and Belmont Street, none of which are currently level with each other. Seventy-eight trees would require to be felled – but they were dying of Dutch Elm disease anyway, so it was put out. In fact only twelve of the seventy-eight trees are elms and even those twelve show little sign of mortal decay.

Sir Ian's team included a number of professional organisations, and ACSEF, (Aberdeen City and Shire Economic Future) a group of local businessmen and the odd councillor, who were to 'spearhead' the venture. ACSEF set about denigrating the Gardens as 'a dark hole that acts as a barrier to the movement of people around the city', while a curious diktat, pronounced 'the City Square Project (as) Aberdeen's last but probably best chance to get the plaza it deserved.'

A public consultation, funded by Scottish Enterprise took place. At a briefing for the city's burgesses, it became apparent that Union Street had been sidelined. Its run down appearance was emphasised. It had had its day. The platform party – Sir Ian and members of ACSEF – were clearly unaware of its seminal importance to Aberdeen's development, the symbolic significance of the relationship of Street and Gardens, its important role in the city's current aspirations. No, Union Street, once an elegant Georgian Street with numerous 'iconic' buildings, six of which are within a matter of yards of Union Terrace Gardens, had been written off.

Illustrations in a booklet accompanying the consultation showed the Square, a large space with people walking about aimlessly on different levels, decorated with imported water features, sculptures and large mature, trees which had apparently managed to grow up though the concrete. The Gardens already have mature trees, several natural levels, and a natural water feature in the Denburn which flows in culvert next to the west side of the railtrack. As for sculptures, directly above the Gardens, Union Terrace offers one of the finest collections of statuary in Britain. 'A thriving cosmopolitan café culture' was represented in the ACSEF booklet by about ten tables surrounded by uncomfortable looking chairs. It is not surprising that all were empty. In one of the pictures, the view of the magnificent Rosemount Viaduct panorama has been reduced to a few lumpish, disembodied turrets. In another the statue of Robbie Burns has been replaced by a sort of elongated Saharan fort. This publication was later withdrawn.

A pull out postcard attached to the booklet allowed one to vote for or against the scheme. It was heavily slanted towards a 'yes' vote and there was little room to indicate reasons for dissent. To quote Norman Marr again: 'I know that some representations made against the scheme were letters on behalf of organisations of 100 or more people – was any cognisance given to this? Also, had the questionnaire been more clearly worded then I believe many more would have come out against the proposal.' In spite of such obstacles the consultation resulted in a vote of 55% against the City Square.

Sir Ian had initially declared that he would let the people of Aberdeen decide, but after they did so in a negative manner, at least from his point of view, he approached the city council for their seal of approval for development in principle. After the ensuing debate, one vote was split fourteen-fourteen with the Lord Provost, contrary to tradition, throwing his casting vote for the City Square rather than the status quo. Later the votes went Byzantine with twenty-seven of forty-three councillors voting for the City Square but with twelve abstentions and four absentees. Make of that what you will. But those Aberdonians whose votes against the Project formed the majority, those who sought to vote but did not know how to go about it, those whose suggestions of less controversial venues were brushed aside, must feel, in varying degrees, a sense of betrayal and regret.

Scarcely a month later on 23 June 2010, before the full Council voted on the proposal, before plans were available for viewing, officials were ready with an agenda for the 'delivery' of the City Garden Project – 'Square' had been dropped – complete with a 'project-management board', a 'strategic, decision-making body providing strategic leadership and overview', a project-management team, a 'design-management company' to find a 'winning vision', and an 'expert jury', to pick the winner. A 'special purpose vehicle' would 'manage the planning and construction phases' while a PR company would 'manage community engagement'. The original completion date of 2014 was extended to allow for possible legal challenges and a public inquiry. This is a wise precaution.

It had been stated by its progentitors that the City Garden Project is necessary to safeguard the future prosperity of the city. Few appear convinced by this declaration. Sir Ian has already stated there will be no commercial development on the Square itself and has added that, 'Below (in the subterranean levels) we could have a two-and-a-half-acre concourse housing an arts centre and facilities for kids, families and people in their late teens and early twenties who don't have any other option at the moment but to hit the pubs at night.' This is a worthy concept, but more akin to a community centre than an El Dorado. The technical appraisal of 'deliverable uses' of the subterranean levels provided by consulting architects Halliday Fraser Munro, indicate more conventional sources of income, for example, a multi-storey car park with 490 spaces on the basement floors. It could serve the redeveloped Triple Kirks and Denburn Health Centre, both on neighbouring sites. On the upper levels, restaurants, cafes, and hotel and conference facilities are cited as a possibility. And, say HFM, there is 'an opportunity to provide a large-size unit (i.e. shop) with frontage to a good secondary retailing pitch on Union Street'. Given the Square's perimeters this can only mean the north side of Union Bridge. Say goodbye to the stunning view across to Rosemount Viaduct, and the last remnant of Union Bridge itself.

Sir Ian's generous benefaction of £50 million came with strings, indeed hawsers, attached. The total cost of the scheme is estimated by ACSEF at £140 million, £90 million of which must come from sources other than Sir Ian – and excluding Aberdeen City Council which has no funds to contribute. The private sector is expected to add £20 million. To make up the £140 million ACSEF hope to borrow the remaining £70 million which will be financed by the anticipated increase in business rates revenue for the area. However a report from the accountants Pricewaterhouse Coopers questions whether the City Square Project would generate enough income to cover the interest on the £70 million loan in its first years. At the usual interest rate of 3%, the loan would cost the city £150 million over a period of twenty-five years. With inevitable escalation, however, the final cost has been put closer to £300 million, with borrowings therefore nearer the £250 million mark. Alex Mitchell of Aberdeen Civic Society writes: 'Sir Ian's £50 million contribution is in reality less of a gift, more of an opportunity to get the city into hock potentially to the extent of £250 million, which at a 5% interest rate would cost the town £12.5 million per annum, all for the sake of a bizarrely oversized and inappropriately located City Square which few of us wanted or saw the point of in the first place'.

The putative £300 million total may be no exaggeration. Among the 'grey areas' the possible handsome and historic demolition of the west side of Belmont Street to 'even up' the levels has not been costed. The engineering problems involved in creating and maintaining a three storey building in a hole in the ground, a natural sump, topped by a vast concrete expanse will be immense. The fate of the Denburn Viaduct at the north end of the Gardens, William Boulton's engineering gem of 1886, under which the railway passes, is unclear. The covering over of the railway line has been costed, but that would be a regrettable step. This part of the North line is the original Denburn Valley Junction Railway which linked the railhead at Kittybrewster and trains from the north with the new Joint Station and trains from the south – hence that station's name. It is part of our railway history. This section of the line offers an enjoyable view of the Gardens. There are already two tunnels a little to the north; passengers do not require a third black-out. At a well-attended picnic in the Gardens in the summer of 2010 everyone enjoyed the sight of the trains running past, and there was much waving between picknickers and passengers. The Gardens were once nicknamed the Trainie Park by local children and their lower level would make an ideal city-centre railway halt. There are numerous ways to make improvements without destruction and without incurring heavy municipal debt. At time of writing, the Battle for Union Terrace Gardens was far from over, though perhaps not. Demonstrators raised concerns about costs prior to a meeting of the full Council at the end of June, and during that meeting some councillors spoke of 'pulling back and saying "no" if the design and finances did not stack up.'

Generally speaking, not a great deal of progress has been made in the improvement or restoration of Union Street since 2008. At the east end, Esslemont & Macintosh's two fine surviving buildings have remained empty since the department store's closure in 2007. A plan to turn both into a 110-bedroom hotel designed by architects Holmes for C&L Properties 'a tremendously exciting project' inevitably with lots of glass, foundered through failure to fined a hotel group to take it on. The buildings have grown increasingly rundown, their weary appearance and crumbling canopies at odds with the fanciful 'Revitalising Aberdeen' posters hopefully plastered over their facades. Now, in a new scheme, Ellis & Wilson's 1887 fine building at No 26-30, originally planned as offices for the *Daily Free Press* and latterly E&M's Ladies' Department may be developed as a forty-bedroom 'boutique' hotel. Across St Catherine's Wynd to the west, at Nos 32-38 (E&M's former Gents' Department), R G Wilson's ornate skyscraper originally designed for the drapers Sangster & Henderson, is planned to become twenty two-bedroom flats.

Further west, next to the old Queen's Cinema, the simple and elegant cabinetmaker's shop of James Allan, latterly a Mothercare branch, was rescued in 2010 from its empty and neglected state by the fashion chain Peacocks. Its cheerful interior resembles what might be a 'boutique' version of the old Littlewoods.

Jamieson & Carry, the jewellers, on the ground floor of Simpson's original Aberdeen Hotel building, have a new frontage, with a brown fascia, modest and dignified, which carries along to include the Victoria Restaurant, still upstairs but owned for some time now by the renowned jewellers.

On the other side of the street, the men's shop Envy at Nos 111-115 was replaced in 2010 by Mountain Warehouse, an outdoor clothing and camping equipment shop. A chain store goes out and a chain store comes in.

Prize for the worst new Union Street frontage must, however, be awarded to SportsDirect.com, the sporting goods company, at the former Boots the Chemists, at

Nos 133-139½. In the early 1930s, Boots received an Art Deco 'makeover' by Geo. Bennett & Sons Architects, stylishly establishing its corporate identity. After the chemists deserted to the Bon Accord Centre, a number of enterprises have presented graceless facades to the passing world; Virgin Megastore, Zavvi, which went bust, and now the afore-mentioned SportsDirect.com, its cheap-looking gigantic billboard style fascia, at odds with the firm's financial success. It seizes passers-by by the throat as they stammer out a protest against the awarding of planning permission to something so inappropriate.

Moving to the west end, the area that once was Union Place looks dismal and unloved. It lies between Summer Street on the north side and Bon Accord Terrace on the south side, and stretches to Holburn Junction The saddest sight is the former Capitol Cinema, whose frontage, once a gleaming Art Deco delight, is now filthy and neglected. Look on it and weep. It was acquired by the Luminar leisure group in 2003 and converted to Jumpin' Jaks and Chicago Rocks nightspots. It was not long before the frontage acquired its shabby and uncleaned look. It closed for 'refurbishment', and later, closed altogether, as Luminar's financial difficulties increased. There are now plans to convert it into an eight or nine storey hotel while the original Art Deco restaurant is to be refurbished. So some good news.

The upper storeys of the former Bell's Hotel next door have as yet lost none of the ambience of the abandoned poorhouse. Like the Capitol, Bell's backs onto Justice Mill Lane, and here a new hotel development is still in the pipe line as it was in 2008, on the site currently occupied by O'Donoghue's Bar. A further two hotels, a Radisson Park Inn and a Travelodge, being built in Justice Mill Lane between the Bon Accord Baths (closed and looking sad) and Strawberry Bank (destroyed), will give four hotels in that area, balancing the proposed developments at the east end, at the former E&M's and the new Ibis Hotel, part of massive City Wharf hotel development near where the Shiprow makes its entry to Union Street. Alas this massive building, part of the current trend for enormity, has blotted out a fine view of the tower of the Harbour Board offices. The cry of under-provision of hotel accommodation in Aberdeen is rapidly changing to one of over-provision. Finally, back in the west end to the very last building on the south side, at one time a rather dreary Chivas Bros and more recently the West End Branch of the Bank of Scotland which went on the market in 2008. The building re-opened in late 2009, metamorphosed into a bright and cheerful Tesco Express, bearing no trace at all of its recent history as a bank.

Diane Morgan, 2010

Union Bridge in the 1830s with, left, the group of buildings around Belmont Street which created an impressive new entrance to the town. The great lum of Provost Hadden's woollen mill rises up from the Green and towers imposingly above the bridge. The Denburn flows below.

THE SECRET WIDENING OF UNION STREET

While I was writing this book I was asked on several occasions to be sure to include the enduring tale of how the width of Union Street was surreptitiously increased, from sixty to seventy feet. The story goes that when the street was under construction, some far-sighted citizens became concerned that it would be too narrow for so important a thoroughfare. One dark night they took the law into their own hands and resourcefully added another ten feet to its width by moving back the alignment pegs. I loved this tale as a child; flaming torches, shadowy figures, the dull thump of mallet on peg, the moon glimpsed between gaps in the fitful cloud.

Alas, all firmly rebutted by learned commentators. In 1965 the historian Fenton Wyness wrote in *City by the Grey North Sea, Aberdeen*, that 'recorded evidence' proved the tale of the secret widening 'to be a complete misrepresentation of facts'. But 'there's aye some watter far the stirkie droons'.

I suspect the 'recorded evidence' that Wyness was referring to is found in Section 2 in the New Streets Act of 4 April 1800, which states that the New Streets (Union Street and King Street) should be '160ft in breadth'. Sixty feet was for the street itself while the remaining one hundred feet, fifty on either side, was reserved for building areas.

In his memoirs of 1897, *Aberdeen Awa*, George Walker tells an interesting tale. When the New Streets Bill was being scrutinised during the committee stage at Westminster, someone, probably Henry Dundas, says Walker, remarked that an additional width of ten feet would make Union Street 'a very splendid street'. It was pointed out that the Bill provided only for a width of sixty feet, but Dundas, 'pooh-pooed it in his despotic way and said it should be disregarded.' On Dundas's comment, so Walker continues, 'an express was instantly sent off by the Aberdeen Committee, (present at Westminster) ordering the deviation pegs, marking the line of the new street be shifted *in the night time*, ten feet wider, which was done.' The powerful parliamentarian Dundas, ('Harry the Ninth, uncrowned King of Scotland'), friend of Pitt the Younger and soon to be created 1st Viscount Melville, had as a young lawyer, given legal advice to Aberdeen Town Council. Noted for his lack of scruples, Dundas appears to have given illegal advice on this occasion. These events were not recorded in the Aberdeen Burgh Records, continues Walker, but all the feu charters are correct as to the increased width.

If this is a true account – and there are questions to be asked - this could not have been the action of a vague group of well-meaning private citizens, but of the very men behind the project, Provost Thomas Leys and his business partner, Provost John Hadden. They had recently built Grandholm Mill in difficult terrain and would develop it into one of Britain's biggest flax mills. Their joint attributes formed an ideal combination to push forward the New Streets project. Hadden was resolute and ruthless, Leys, a man of vision, cultured, far-sighted and able. They were the sort of men for whom 'a very splendid street' was a *sine qua non*. They were now working at virtual government level, in cahoots with Dundas who was unlikely to have made such important utterances about the street spontaneously.

There were those in Aberdeen who thought the future Union Street project, a great road stretching above the cosy confines of the small medieval town, particularly over-ambitious. Anticipating increased opposition from the faint-hearted, and the waste of time and money in having the New Streets Bill amended, especially when work had already begun (albeit a trifle prematurely) the Hadden-Leys faction simply got on with the surreptitious peg shifting. Physically it was not an easy task to carry out in darkness but Hadden's great woollen mill down in the Green would have made an ideal base for organising 'a parcel of men' - a gang of labourers – and handing out the tools.

The affair had the Hadden stamp. Sixteen years later, just after he had completed his third stint as provost, he assembled great gangs of men, kitted them out with tools purloined from the Harbour Trustees and 'under cloud of night' urged them on to alter the course of the River Don and to dig the Persley lade wide and deep enough take six times more water than before. And so he increased the flow of water to Grandholm Mill and with it, its productive capacity. Compared with that, ten feet more to Union Street was small beer.

INTRODUCTION

In the early nineteenth century it was very different from today. Union Bridge with its massive, airy span was one of the wonders of a gracious age. Union Street, with the harmony of its architecture and the symmetry of its fine terraces, was dazzling. It was largely the work of the great architects, Archibald Simpson and John Smith, Aberdonians both. They were inspired by the simple, neoclassical styles, based on the architecture of ancient Greece and Rome that were highly fashionable throughout Europe, which could be worked up beautifully in the white granite that was conveniently available out at the Dancing Cairns. Along with Regent Street in London and Grey Street in Newcastle-upon-Tyne, Union Street was hailed as one of the finest thoroughfares in Britain. There was great local pride in its magnificence.

The new street, devised to improve access to the town, did much more. It provided the impetus and the locus for a new city built over the cramped medieval burgh. It was the linchpin in a brilliant traffic system that has served us well for years and which still links with four out of five of the original turnpike roads, those arriving from the south, from Deeside and from Skene at Holburn Junction, and the Ellon turnpike coming in from the north at King Street. Only the Inverurie route, arriving via George Street/St Nicholas Street, has been blocked off.

From its early days Union Street was busy. Although it was intended originally as a residential area, upwardly mobile local retailers quickly left the likes of Broad Street and the Gallowgate in the old town and colonised the ground floors of the new houses, even whole buildings. Union Street developed a wide range of excellent shops and became a shoppers' paradise. The city's leading lawyers, architects and accountants took up residence on the first floors, as did several small schools and numerous insurance companies, their names in huge brass lettering affixed to the outer walls of their premises. In the upper levels were music and singing teachers, artists' studios, small hotels, caretakers and ordinary residents. Tailors and seamstresses who made up garments for the legions of Union Street clothiers were tucked away on upper or lower floors. As the years passed, light industries flourished nearby, in Union Row and Rose Street. Aberdeen University and R G I T, the future Robert Gordon University, were both based near the city centre and their students added vitality to Union Street life. From the early twentieth century, five, later six Union Street cinemas offered continuous performances, with a constant coming and going of patrons.

Something was always happening even if it were just the tram driver dismounting at Holburn Junction to change the points, or the hunchbackit man playing the accordion outside Woolworth's. If he were ever away, the place seemed curiously empty. Mary Garden, the great opera singer, would occasionally make a continuous grand entrance along Union Street. Entrances of a different kind were made by fish or factory workers, usually on a Friday, just prior to their nuptials. They would be seized by workmates, divested of most of their clothes, covered with soot, thrown into the back of a lorry and driven up and down Union Street while their tormentors clanged and banged away with various utensils. I realised later that this was the ancient ceremony of blacking, or at least a modern version. It was quite terrifying for a child.

It was a great place for parades. Rare sightings of the Dons triumphant on their open-topped bus were guaranteed to bring out the whole town. The Torcher was vivid and exciting, even scary, and bore no resemblance to the present anaemic procession, girt round by the embargoes of Health and Safety legislation. Prior to being amalgamated, the local regiment, the Gordon Highlanders, exercised their right to march down Union Street with bayonets fixed, drums beating and colours flying as they had done in the past. This was a heart-wrenching occasion as most onlookers had links with the Regiment. Men in the crowd were wearing their medals, and there were tears in many eyes.

This Union Street that many of us knew has gone, diminished over the years by a series of untoward events. In 1958, fifty years ago as I write, the trams formed their own sad cortège, gliding toward shameful incineration at the Beach. Their curiously comforting whirr, whoosh and clanking was stilled forever. The cinemas closed, thanks to TV and bingo. The universities consolidated on the outskirts, and the 'buzz' and spending power of their students went with them. The light industries retreated to the new industrial zones. Then came unnecessary demolitions and the intrusion of unsympathetic and architecturally inferior buildings in the name of redevelopment in the very heart of Union Street. The fact that it is the city's prime conservation area, containing numerous listed buildings, appeared to carry little weight. Supermarkets were arriving in residential areas, providing the parking that Union Street lacked. Shops that were household names began to quit. The 'soulless malls' opened, apparently beloved of no one but their progenitors and P R men, but warm, clean and offering convenient parking all the same.

The St Nicholas and Bon Accord Centres were especially dangerous. Though it was known that major Union Street stores planned to relocate there, no serious thought seems to have been given to the side effects of this exodus – an epidemic of empty buildings and an eventual legacy of mobile-phone shops, computer-games shops, mortgage shops, property shops, takeaways, bookies and charity shops – though the latter remain one of the few places where serious attempts at window-dressing are made and where people can enjoy a good rummage. Now only three Union Street shops are locally owned: Jamieson & Carry, Michie's and Bruce Miller. Managers of multiples who are moved to Aberdeen, say for a two-year period, cannot be expected to have the same commitment to the street as a local, nor indeed can distant landlords.

Added to these setbacks, Union Street was showing its age. In 1800, the parliamentary 'go ahead' was given, and the ensuing construction of the street took place in 1801–5. The millennium of 2000 fell around the time of the street's bicentenary. An ideal time, therefore, to seek millennium funding to carry out a reinstatement of a unique Georgian street. Even starting modestly with mandatory colour schemes and the restoration of dilapidated dormers would have given a foretaste of just what could be done. But the opportunity was never grasped, perhaps never even considered.

And so, instead of having a master plan dedicated to its own future, Union Street has been marginalised to facilitate other policies. Current licensing policy, for example, encourages ever more pubs to locate in its west end, presumably so that the bobbies can more easily corral drunken hooligans, though leaving the street vulnerable to vandalism and rendering it a no-go area for non-inebriates. Another policy is to pedestrianise its eastern half, the Bridge Street to Market Street section, but this is traffic policy. I'm not sure of its aim, but it will further isolate the north end of the city, already cut off by the positioning of the Bon Accord Centre across George Street and the closing of Justice Street at the Castlegate. Built as a major thoroughfare, Union Street does not have the cosy ambience of a pedestrian precinct, nor, to be frank, the weather, nor the shops. Nor, since it was engineered as a viaduct in the crucial area, does it have a handy grid of neighbouring streets onto which to decant traffic.

There are bright spots. Some recent frontages are a considerable improvement on past efforts (though I wish shops would include their street numbers) and a few quality clothes shops and coffee shops have moved into the central area and the west end. But the street is nowhere near fulfilling its potential. Take the relatively recent metamorphosis of a large church into a café-bar. It was a good conversion, but at the end of the day, it remains another pub among many. What an interesting change to have had a mini House of Bruar, a Millers or Morgan McVeigh's instead, using the great height of the church spectacularly to accommodate galleries of shops selling everything from antiques and overcoats to cheeses and caviar.

If anyone is running Union Street at all, I suspect it must be men in suits. It is time it was run by ladies in hats provided, of course, they are as formidable as they are charming, are trained as architects or art historians, have a love of real shopping, are *au fait* with the inner workings of the rag trade and are not inclined to be overwhelmed by aspiring developers. They would ban all window-dressing that was confined to posters about mortgages, interest rates or loans, or endless displays of houses for sale; they would dispatch the guzzling, shrieking lunchtime hordes back to their school dinners, strike down garish, oversized fascias and dingy meaningless banners, dispose of ugly and unnecessary street 'furniture' and dispense soap and water to those owners whose premises required it.

But *The Granite Mile*, outwith this Introduction, is not a girn about drinks culture, mismanagement or the triumph of philistinism, nor entirely a *recherche du temps perdu*. The first chapter describes the street's intensive labour pains, the others take the form of a stroll along the entire length. These seven sections can be read in any order. Hopefully this journey will bring back happy memories, and the buildings may surprise you. Many are still stunning. Union Street is a priceless inheritance and *The Granite Mile* may inspire some discussion about how we can give it the future it deserves.

Diane Morgan 2008

The grand entrance to the New Market a few yards from Union Street. It stopped Sir John Betjeman in his tracks when he visited Aberdeen in 1947. 'So bold, so simple in design, so colossal in proportion,' he said, 'I had seen nothing like it before or since.'

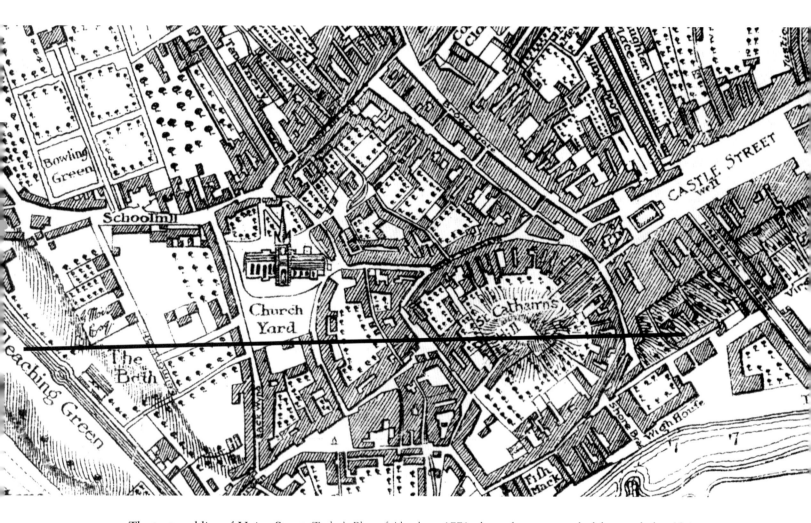

The proposed line of Union Street. *Taylor's Plan of Aberdeen, 1771, shows the eastern end of the area before Union Street existed. It would run from the south-west end of Castle Street, right, across the top of St Catherine's Hill, past the churchyard, where Correction and Back Wynds can be seen to the right and left respectively of the church (St Nicholas Kirk), then on to the Denburn Ravine at the Beaching Green, left, and so, finally, across the western plain.*

CHAPTER ONE

THE BUILDING OF
UNION STREET

'A Great and Lasting Improvement'

The Magistrates and Council of Aberdeen, 23 September 1817

It had rained all morning. But when the procession set out from the Castlegate at one o'clock, on Tuesday, 7 July 1801, the downpour ceased abruptly. The dignitaries might not, after all, have to wring the water out of their coat tails. In the time-honoured phrase, 'Abidy wis there'. Leading the procession were members of all the city's Mason Lodges, with the band of the Fifeshire militia behind them providing a selection of martial airs. There followed the Principals and Professors of King's and Marischal Colleges, at that time separate universities, and the city ministers, all of them recognisable by their assortment of hoods, gowns and Geneva bands. The architect, David Hamilton, although he came from Glasgow, and was therefore unknown to locals, could also be easily picked out for, in the traditional style, he carried his plans in his hand. With him walked the surveyor, Charles Abercrombie. Insiders murmured that the pair were in league. Then came Alexander Allardyce, member of Parliament for Aberdeen Burghs, and the city magistrates. Among them was Thomas Leys of Glasgoforest, provost from 1797–8, and a moving spirit behind the mighty undertaking that was about to be inaugurated. 'A great concourse of people' took up the rear.

The procession went by way of Broad Street, the Upperkirkgate and the Schoolhill, then turned down the Denburn Walk, a narrow path replaced more recently and at a higher level by the Denburn dual carriageway. At this spot, the Denburn, a busy waterway that made its way from Kingswells in the west, through the town to the primitive harbour, entered the great ravine of the Denburn Valley, known locally as the 'Den'. Nearby, the housewives and washerwomen at the common bleachfield (now the lowest level of Union Terrace Gardens) paused in their tasks to observe the goings-on. The procession had slowed down and the purpose of the ceremony became clear. The foundation stone of 'the new bridge over the

Denburn' – which would not only cross the burn, but link both sides of the ravine – was about to be laid, with full Masonic honours. This was not some arcane ritual, but normal procedure for the foundation ceremonies of new building projects. Stonemasons, after all, would play a major role in the work to come.

Provost John Dingwall presided (lord provosts were not invented until 1863). He was also, appropriately, Master of the Ancient Lodge of Aberdeen Freemasons. In his speech, he referred to the praises which Alexander Allardyce, MP, the previous speaker, had heaped on Thomas Leys. 'I cannot omit this opportunity,' he said, 'in joining you in the just eulogium you have bestowed upon the exertions of my worthy predecessor Mr Leys, who has, by his perseverance and zeal, contributed so essentially to bring this work to its present advanced state.'

At the end of the ceremony, the heavens opened and the on-ding resumed with greater ferocity than ever. The brief but opportune respite from the elements was hailed, incorrectly as it transpired, as an auspicious sign.

The story of Union Street began about ten years earlier. The lawyer and historian, William Kennedy, later summarised the situation in his *Annals of Aberdeen* of 1818: 'While the nation was engaged in the late tedious war [against Napoleon], Aberdeen enjoyed peace and tranquillity at home,' he wrote. 'Its shipping, commerce and manufactures had greatly increased, far beyond expectation. From these sources as well as from the produce of the county, an influx of wealth soon became manifest.'

What now concerned Aberdonians above all else, Kennedy explained, was the state of the roads leading to the town centre, particularly Castle Street or the Castlegate (both names were used then as now) a noble square with handsome buildings and a unique and impressive market cross. Unfortunately, with the exception of the Broadgate or Broad Street as it was increasingly being called the approach roads were 'crooked, narrow, tortuous and hilly, fit only for pack horses' and 'long a subject of complaint'.

Travellers to Aberdeen from the south, after crossing the Dee, came via the Hardgate, providing they could find it, then down Windmill Brae, along the Green, then up the Shiprow and into the Castlegate. Those from the north came via the Brig o' Balgownie, Old Aberdeen, the Spital, the Mounthooly marshes and the Gallowgate, the worst road in the country, so it was said. 'It is with great difficulty that a stranger can find his way either in or out,' commented the Glasgow surveyor, Charles Abercrombie. Matters were complicated by the city's growing population. In 1755 it stood at 10,488; by 1795 it had risen to 16,120.

'Improvements,' wrote Kennedy, 'became an object of general attention'. One obvious improvement for this prosperous but overcrowded town, constrained by its cramped medieval streets and its appalling approaches, was expansion towards the sparsely populated plain to the west, the area from Diamond Street to Holburn Junction in modern times meant that the formidable Denburn ravine had to be bridged.

In 1794, Charles Abercrombie was working on a turnpike road system for the County of Aberdeen landowners who, as turnpike trustees, would become responsible for the funding and management of these new roads. Since he was in the area, it was appropriate that the city magistrates should invite him to inspect Aberdeen itself and suggest ways of improving access. His report, datelined 'Glasgow, December 1794' and addressed 'to the Honourable the Magistrates of the City of Aberdeen', called for 'wide and direct streets ... [and] by that means the Town can be greatly enlarged, and in place of being one of the most irregular, may become one of the most regular Towns in the Kingdom'.

Of three new approaches suggested by Abercrombie, his own favourite was a 'direct elevated street' linking the Castlegate and 'the extensive plain to the west of the town'. Stand on that same 'extensive plain' of a quiet Sunday morning – Holburn Junction is a good vantage point – and look east. Far off, one sees the Castlegate and the start of Union Street, with a slight dip around the Market Street junction, a gentle rise as the street runs westwards, then a levelling out. It was not, perhaps, too difficult for Abercrombie to create a modern street from whatever was there before – a rough track perhaps?

Nothing could be further from the truth. There was no road there. The Castlegate was shut off at its west end by 'a big block of common-looking houses with shops on the ground floor', according to the nineteenth-century historian, William Robbie. Exit at this end was only by Narrow Wynd leading north to Broad Street, and by the future Exchequer Row, leading south to the Shiprow. Immediately west of the 'common-looking houses' loomed the mass of St Catherine's Hill, heavily populated round its lower slopes. Round its southern and eastern flanks wound the ancient Shiprow. At the foot of the western slopes, the slum settlements of Putachieside and Carnegie's Brae were scattered. Beyond St Catherine's Hill, the ground was crossed by the Correction and Back Wynds, respectively on the east and west sides of St Nicholas Kirk, both heading for the Green. Belmont Street, to the west, was in the course of being laid out to meet the Green, though it never did. Further west, the ground ran down to the 'Den', then rose to higher ground, at the Doocot Brae, the present Union Terrace Gardens.

'I propose crossing the "Den" by a Bridge of three arches,' and then cutting about fifteen feet of St Catherine's Hill and arching the winds [Wynds] between it and the Den,' Abercrombie's Report announced. This was a bold proposal and George Walker in his memoirs, *Aberdeen Awa'*, (1897) tells us that Abercrombie took 'advantage of the suggestions of a woolcomber in Provost Leys's employment whose rough drafts were submitted to him', and apparently embraced them as his own.

'Arching the winds'. Correction Wynd has been arched over. Our cyclist is leaving Correction Wynd at the Green end to cycle under Union Street.

Though the Report was not yet public, rumours must have spread. Townsfolk who knew of Abercrombie's plan were staggered at its audacity. The cost of purchasing, purely for demolition, all the buildings on the St Catherine's Hill slopes, Putachieside (the future Market Street area) and the Wynds and others that lay in the way of the proposed route, starting with the 'common-looking houses' at the Castlegate, would be immense. Cutting fifteen feet from the north shoulder of St Catherine's Hill was a huge, labour-intensive task and – like all the demolition and construction involved in this massive project – would have to be accomplished by pick and shovel. To maintain the correct level of the 'direct elevated street', the ground between the west end of the Castlegate to the Doocot Brae, and beyond, to the future Diamond Street, would take the form of a viaduct, built up by retaining walls or arches of brick, most of which would be 'blind', that is, covered in earth. The climax of the elevated street would be the building of a great bridge over the Denburn ravine. This explains why early commentaries on the project are concerned with Union Bridge rather than Union Street. Its easterly section was the bridge's approach road.

Abercrombie says little in his Report about the skills demanded for the creation of the new street, but stresses how the council's financial outlay could be recovered. This may have been part of his brief. He explains, for example, that 'in place of banking where the ground is hollow I would propose to arch it all the way, divide in the middle of the street, lay out the space created as cellars … which could be let out by the Council to the proprietors on either side. This in a good measure will pay the expence [sic] in execution.' 'Street on Vaults', was, in fact, one of the names given to the project. Similarly, 'by a regular plan', he divided the western plain, between the present Union Terrace Gardens and Holburn Junction, into building lots to produce revenue for the council from the sale of feus.

This, the first arch under Union Street, *is in fact a tunnel which goes underground at Carnegie's Brae at the rear of Marks & Spencer, crosses Union Street and the top of Market Street and emerges in the East Green.*

After reading Abercrombie's Report and mulling over the implications, the Town Council took no immediate action. Eventually, after a year and more had passed, the city's enterprising police commissioners decided to nudge the council into action. Thanks largely to the determination of John Ewen, a wealthy Castlegate merchant and silversmith, Aberdeen had taken policing powers in 1795. Ewen, a, patron of the arts, dedicated burgh reformer, Friend of the French Revolution, apocryphal author of *The Boatie Rows* and pioneer of bathing machines at the Beach, did much to bring Aberdeen into the nineteenth century. 'Policing' was not what we mean today, though the derivation – from *polis*, the Greek word for a city – is the same. It included responsibility for paving, lighting, water supply and cleansing of the borough, duties carried out by police commissioners who were a parallel authority to the town council. But while the council was a self-electing, nepotistic oligarchy (in spite of Ewen's best efforts, burgh reform was still thirty years away), the police commissioners were forward-looking men with an electorate to answer to. An important part of their remit was improving the streets within the city and the roads and avenues within the royalty (roughly, the outskirts). Although the Police Board did not formally come into being until after Abercrombie's report was written, they were much concerned with it. In March 1796, they presented the magistrates with a memorial (petition), clearly with the report in mind, urging the need to adopt a route 'terminating so favourably as to combine excellency of free, short and easy access to the harbour and market place' (the Castlegate). Such a road would open communication to the south, 'including the farthest extremities of Great Britain'. The police commissioners were not lacking in ambition for the city.

The following month, Abercrombie's Report had an airing at a meeting of the trustees of the turnpike roads of the County of Aberdeen, who recommended it to the magistrates for their consideration. The latter could not continue to ignore the urgings of bodies as important as the police commissioners and the turnpike trustees, so a meeting was convened on 29 July to consider the report. Kennedy noted that they were 'averse to embark on so serious an undertaking', concerned that the raising of what inevitably would be 'such a large sum of Money' was apparently to come mainly from loans and subscriptions rather than by taxation. In hindsight, the magistrates' caution was commendable. However, they were willing to listen to any plan, providing it wasn't too costly, and decided to confer with 'the gentlemen of the county'.

At last, on 26 February 1799, the increasingly impatient police commissioners called a general meeting of the citizens, or at least those with the requisite property qualifications to vote for them – that is, men in possession of property rated annually at £5 sterling. The meeting was ostensibly to discuss increasing the local 'rate of assessment' – the rates. It was known that other business involving more fundamental change would be discussed, and there was a great turnout of the duly qualified, from gentlemen to tradesmen, among them Andrew Jopp, advocate; Adam Watt, baker; Mr Martin of Nellfield; Patrick Scott, mason; Dr Dauney; John Garvock, staymaker; Charles Lunan, watchmaker; John Clark, flax-dresser; gentry, university professors, lawyers, provosts (a title retained for life by former provosts), magistrates, merchants, booksellers, shoemakers, fleshers, glaziers and ale-sellers.

Thomas Leys was invited to take the chair in his capacity as chief magistrate, and he chaired all the momentous meetings that followed. In 1788, at the age of twenty-four, Leys had inherited his father's wealth and his estate of Glasgoforest in Kinellar parish. Leys Snr was an Aberdeen baillie and flax-manufacturer and Thomas, with his brother-in-law, Alexander Brebner of Learney, and his colleague James Hadden, both future provosts, expanded the family firm, Leys, Masson & Co, into one of Britain's major linen manufacturers. They built the great mill at Grandholm in almost inaccessible terrain, on the River Don opposite Woodside. Having contributed £500, Leys was one of the top subscribers to the Inverurie turnpike, which ran alongside his estate and through Woodside which was then largely owned by Leys Masson. The new Aberdeenshire Canal ran a similar course. Perhaps not unexpectedly, Leys was both a prominent member of the turnpike committee, and chairman of the Canal Company. With his experience of business, of building and road-making techniques, of man-management, with his ability to handle the warring factions on these various committees, with his youth, energy and enthusiasm, it is no surprise to learn that Leys was the moving spirit behind the creation of Union Street during his first provostship and its building during his second stint in 1803–4.

Abercrombie's scheme was not only approved at the meeting of February 1799, but a committee of thirty-six gentlemen was appointed then and there 'to consider altering and enlarging the old roads opening up new ones and getting plans and estimates'. On 1 July 1799, the committee of thirty-six reported that they had commissioned a local surveyor, Colin Innes, to provide 'an actual and accurate survey' of the 'two new avenues proposed' ie, the future Union Street, and the future King Street as well. These streets would not only be commodious, but also adapted for extending, opening up and beautifying the town. That was important. The prevailing philosophy was that streets and buildings must be beautiful as well as practical. The committee had walked the line of both avenues with Innes. However, visions of Aberdeen's thirty-six most prominent citizens scrambling up hill and down dale, wigs askew and breeches covered in mud are unrealistic, given that the quorum was thirteen and they probably rode. The July meeting was unanimous: the two roads were now to go ahead. As Kennedy reported: 'Matters were now in the hands of the community.'

At the third meeting of the citizens in September 1799, the committee reported that Abercrombie had been back in town, that they had got estimates from him – far too low as it transpired – and that a Bill had been drafted to go before Parliament, which would give official authority to purchase properties along the route. As it was, Aberdeen's magistrates, foreseeing the inevitability of the new roads, had already been quietly buying up properties on the proposed line. This Bill became 'the New Streets Act' on 4 April 1800. Section 1 stated that Union Street was to be laid out, not from the Bridge of Dee, as Abercrombie had initially planned, but less ambitiously, 'beginning at a footpath or lane leading from the entry of the Damhead Road towards the Chapel of Ease'. This sounds obscure, but in modern terms it is roughly the area around Summer Street, at its junction with Gilcomston South Church, a well known road juncture of the time.

Section 20 stipulated that the sum of £15,000 had to be raised by the trustees by 'subscription, loan or otherwise' before any construction on the south street could begin. Trustees were appointed to oversee the work, meeting quarterly. These were nominated from the ranks of the magistrates and members of Parliament, and included the Principal of Marischal College, the President of the Society of Advocates, the Convener of the Seven Incorporated Trades, and the President of the Society of Shipmasters.

In the first instance, all remaining property which lay in the projected path of the future new streets had now to be purchased for demolition. Among the proprietors to be compensated were the wealthy merchant, Patrick Milne of Crimonmogate; James Elmslie, a Midmar mason; and James Massie, wright and builder, in whose Castlehill office Archibald Simpson, the great architect of Union Street, was placed as a fourteen-year-old to learn something of his future calling. At the end of 1800 'offers of sale' had been received from seventy-three owners on the line of the future Union Street. There was no compulsory purchase in those days. It was a sellers' market, as Kennedy pointed out:

> the proprietors of houses and grounds in the lines of the intended streets availed themselves of the opportunity of enhancing the value of their properties far beyond the original estimate.

How unsporting! Though the trustees sold the down-takings to contractors, the income from this source was modest.

The trustees also advertised in the press, inviting architects to submit plans for the new scheme. Out of seven entrants, David Hamilton, like Abercrombie, a Glasgow man, was

Work goes ahead *on Union Bridge at last, with lum-hatted Thomas Fletcher in charge. The future Union Terrace Gardens can be seen through the arch of the Bridge.*

chosen. His sketches were an elaboration and expansion on Abercrombie's original theme of a 'Street on Vaults', with a three-span bridge over the 'Den' with two sets of stairs leading down to the Denburn. Thomas Fletcher, engineer, was appointed to supervise the work. He had recently overseen the building of the Aberdeenshire Canal under the renowned John Rennie, the consulting engineer. Both would have been well known to Thomas Leys, Chairman of the Aberdeenshire Canal Company.

And so the foundation stone of the 'Grand Arch over the Denburn' was laid with great pomp as related. These mighty roadworks were subsequently named Union Street and Union Bridge to commemorate the Union of Great Britain and Ireland on 1 January 1801, an event of national importance. Thus a point was made. Here was no mere parochial undertaking, but a 'landmark' bridge. The north avenue, King Street, in honour of George III, was contemporaneous with Union Street, but was completed without major topographical problems.

Four masons had contracted to complete the work on Union Bridge in a year, but after about nine months it was clear that they had got their financial calculations badly wrong. They were permitted to give up the contract, having laid only the foundations and the piers. Equally disturbing was the discovery by Thomas Fletcher of errors in David Hamilton's levels.

Union Bridge in 1807, *looking south to the Bow Brig, from the watercolour by Robert Seaton presented to Provost Leys and the Trustees by Thomas Fletcher. In 1801, the procession would have walked along the path, extreme left, to lay the foundation stone. The site of the future Union Terrace Gardens, at this time a common bleaching green, is on the right.*

Hamilton's design was abandoned and John Rennie, who replaced him, submitted three alternative designs. Thomas Telford was in the area and Provost James Hadden decided to take advice from him, late in 1801. The great man gave his approval, not to any of Rennie's designs, but to one submitted by Thomas Fletcher, Rennie's second-in-command at the Canal. It proposed a granite bridge with a single span of 130 feet, graceful, yet economical. And so the Glasgow mafia of Abercrombie and Hamilton was superseded, dare one say, by the Aberdeenshire Canal coterie of Leys and Fletcher. As for Rennie, his nose was not too far out of joint. He had already started work on the soon-to-be famous Kelso Bridge of 1803, his prototype for the first Waterloo Bridge over the Thames.

Work now proceeded without further mischanter and the keystone was driven in on 25 August 1803. Eighteen months later, the bridge and its approaches were virtually complete and the *Aberdeen Journal* was able to report that on Saturday, 23 February, 'a gentleman on horseback passed along the line of Union Street and crossed the Grand Arch over the Denburn on his way out of town'.

The bridge was formally opened on 4 June 1805, when the mail coach 'elegantly decorated' and the guard and postillions in gleaming new livery left town for the first time 'by that noble arch', ornamented with a stone parapet and balustrade of highly dressed granite, designed by James Burn of Haddington. He was the architect of the handsome new headquarters for the Aberdeen Banking Company at the top of Marischal Street (now a courthouse). When creating the Union Bridge balustrade, Burn simply repeated his design for the parapet from the roof of the bank. The bridge was indeed a noble arch. It was the widest span in the country for a time, ranking with Edinburgh's North Bridge and with Rennie's Kelso Bridge. It combined the important criteria of beauty and usefulness.

Aberdonians took immense pride in its elegance and splendour, and numerous contemporary prints featured Union Bridge from all angles. One watercolour of the bridge by the local artist Robert Seaton, dated 1805, was presented by Thomas Fletcher to Provost Leys and his Trustees. The inscription reads:

> To Thomas Leys Esquire of Glasgoforest, Provost of Aberdeen and the other Trustees appointed by Act of Parliament for making two new Streets in that City; This North view of the Bridge of Granite Stone built by them over Denburn Valley in the line of Union Street is most respectfully inscribed by their most obedient humble Servant Tho Fletcher Civil Engineer and Superintendent of the public Improvements carried on under their Direction. Span of the Arch 130 feet Rise 29 feet Heighth [sic] of the Bridge from the ground to the carriageway 46 feet Carriageway 40 feet.

Fletcher, ever the engineer, had squeezed the dimensions in as an afterthought around the last couple of lines of the dedication. The forty-foot carriageway, reduced to that size on Thomas Telford's instructions, would cause problems in the future.

The uptake of Union Street feus was disappointing. They were expensive and carried with them demanding building regulations. Between the Castlegate and Union Bridge, for example, buildings of no more than four storeys were permitted, and had to be of granite stone, dressed at least as well as the Athenaeum. (This was not the Athenaeum we know, not yet in existence, but Provost Brown's earlier building of the same name in Exchequer Row.) To bring in much-needed revenue, inducements were offered to those planning to build 'west of the Denburn'. In February 1804 Thomas Leys, as a New Street Trustee and Provost, wrote to the Deacon of the Hammermen stating that:

> it will be for the interest of all concerned that the restrictions to be imposed upon the different proprietors and feuars should be as few as possible. With this view, they (the New Street Trustees) propose that the only limitations in regard to the buildings shall be that 'the front houses between each opening or cross street … shall form one compartment and be of the same height of forewall, number of floors and pitch of roof. And that the whole shall be built of well-dressed granite stone. They also propose that the front walls shall be retired eight feet from each side of the street to form a sunk floor or area of that breadth, having an iron railing towards the street which will be found not only very convenient and useful but will tend much to beautify the street itself.
>
> I flatter myself that these proposals are so reasonable that no person can gave the least objection to them.
>
> I am sir, your most obedient servant,
>
> Thomas Leys, Provost

This accounts for the railings, now virtually all gone, which were once such feature of Union Street beyond Union Bridge. The street also gained in elegance along its entire length from the arcading effect, created by matching arched windows, doors and entrances. Uniformity was de rigueur and it created a wonderful symmetry.

A few years later Provost Leys died, still only in his forties. Aside from his numerous ongoing commitments, he was convener of the County of Aberdeen at the time, in itself a demanding undertaking. By then, it had become obvious that incentives such as remission of the first year's feu duty were having little effect on the city treasury. Aberdeen's descent towards a financial black hole must have been apparent to Leys, causing him considerable concern. In *Aberdeen Awa'*, George Walker summed up his contribution to the creating of Union Street:

> Nine persons out of ten give the credit of initiating these improvements to Provost James Hadden … But the nine persons are wrong, for although he worked energetically and ably in carrying them out, it is to the fine taste and discriminating foresight of Provost Leys of Glasgoforest that we are mainly indebted for their conception and commencement although dying in 1809, he did not live to see their completion.

He was also spared the trauma of the city's insolvency. By 1817, twelve years after the gentleman on horseback crossed the Grand Arch over the Denburn for the first time, only one row of buildings had gone up on the south side of the street, from the Shiprow to Putachieside (the future Market Street), a couple of houses on the north side, and Crimonmogate's House west of Union Bridge. Civic outlays had been enormous. The expense of making the two New Streets, building bridges, sewers, retaining walls, etc., came to £34,422, with Union Street taking the lion's share, greatly in excess of Abercrombie's original estimates. The buying-in of houses for demolition had cost £73,163 4s 5d, more than twice the estimated £30,000. In addition, administration costs including work in connection with the Act of Parliament came to over £6,000. Additional outlay at this time for the Bridewell in Rose Street, harbour improvements and contributions towards the new turnpike road to Stonehaven had cost the town a further £63,000. In order to expedite this work and particularly the New Streets Scheme, the city treasurer had borrowed heavily. The accumulated interest on loans stood at £57,000 while the city's overall deficit was £225,710 14s 4d.

The Treasurer suspended interest payments on loans, the city was bankrupt and by 21 February the insolvent council had conveyed all the burgh's property to twenty-one trustees appointed to represent the creditors. There followed a vicious period of civic squabbling and recrimination, during which all parties involved blamed each other. Throughout these troubles, the trustees were not prepared to accept the 'quick fix' of a lowering of building standards. It is owing to their stubbornness, their refusal to compromise, that we have what is still a fine street.

By 1824, the period of insolvency was to all intents and purposes over. Civic coffers were filling, Union Street likewise and grand new schemes were in the offing.

UNION BUILDINGS.

The first sketch of the Union Buildings. *Baillie Galen's third of the building is to the right; Provost Brown's two-thirds are to the left, and include the roof panel with swag decoration.*

CHAPTER TWO

FROM THE ATHENAEUM
TO THE QUEEN*

'The Athenaeum, which was one of the first buildings erected in Union Street, of which my father was a member, and to which he sometimes took me that I might look at the *Illustrated London News*, with instructions not to talk.'

Lachlan Mackinnon, Recollections of an Old Lawyer, 1935

The South Side: The Union Buildings and the Athenaeum

Union Street begins with the Union Buildings, which run from the Castlegate to where the Shiprow enters Union Street. The address of this island site was initially Nos 1–21 Union Buildings; in 1913 they were absorbed as Nos 1–21 Union Street. Today the whole building is called the Athenaeum, though originally, that was preserved for the magnificent Castlegate façade. They were built between 1819–22 by the architect Archibald Simpson, an early Union Street work, but not his first. Baillie Galen, a relative by marriage, was the client. He owned the westerly feu of this three-feu site where the 'common-looking buildings' once sat, before most were taken down to make way for Union Street. But the remnant of these buildings, not required for demolition, still stood at the Castlegate end. That particular 'common-looking building' was the bow-fronted shop of the merchant and police commissioner, John Ewen.

Simpson therefore began work on at the west end. He gave the block a gently curving end to match that of the already completed Nos 23–49, forming an elegant entrance to Union Street for the Shiprow, still at that time much used as an entry into Aberdeen. The first section, constructed by 1819, contained a first-floor apartment for Baillie Galen at No 19, entered by a stair at the Shiprow end, leading to his spacious sitting room. There were other apartments above, and the ground floor, No 21, was occupied by Archibald's brother's shop, Simpson & Whyte, clothiers.

* *Not Her Majesty in person, but the bronze statue of 1893 by C. B. Birch which gave its name to this once popular meeting place at the Union Street – St Nicholas Street corner. The statue was moved to the Queen's Cross Roundabout in 1964.*

Union Buildings stood incomplete for three years until John Ewen died and his bow-fronted shop was demolished. Simpson then completed the Castle Street façade, strikingly different from the Union Street frontage. Why should this be? The answer lies with Alexander Brown, a local bookseller who had set up his Athenaeum Reading Room and Library across in Exchequer Row. By 1820 this Athenaeum was due for demolition, but Brown had bought the east and centre feus of the Union Buildings site, and was determined that his new Athenaeum Newsroom should do Union Street proud. The great east-facing windows, overlooking the Castlegate, were designed for practicality as well as show, catching as much daylight as possible for the convenience of readers, for whom an impressive list of newspapers and magazines was available. The building cost him 'well on to £12,000' and the feu duty at £375 8s per annum was very high. The city, however, was still bankrupt at this time, in desperate need of income from Union Street feus and Brown, who would become provost in 1822, doubtless felt he was doing a public duty.

The new Athenaeum Newsroom did not pay its way. The structure of the high reading room 'cut the building up in such a manner as to render it unprofitable as a paying investment', as George Walker wrote in *Aberdeen Awa'*. Meanwhile a new reading room which had subsequently opened in the County Buildings (later the Music Hall) proved to be a costly rival. But Brown struggled on for twenty years, before famously selling the Newsroom to its attendant, James Blake, for £5. Blake continued there until 1867, when the building was commandeered for courtrooms while the new Town House and sheriff courts were being erected across the road.

The ground and upper floors of the Union Buildings housed names long remembered in the city. Among them were Arthur Clyne, architect, A & R Milne, booksellers, Keith & Gibb, lithographers, and George Pegler, greengrocer. Archibald Simpson's brother's shop remained at No 21 Union Buildings until 1906, though Sandy Simpson and Baillie Whyte had long passed on. The Dundee Equitable (DE) Boot Depot moved in, flitting the short distance from No 27 Union Street (now Oddbins), where it had been based since the 1880s. The DE, now in its fifth generation of ownership by the Smith family, is still at No 21 as the 'Foot Factory'.

James Hay arrived at the Union Buildings in 1878. He was a shrewd man, a great wit and a first-class restaurateur. He had learnt his trade along at the Royal Hotel, from David Robertson, last of Aberdeen's coaching innkeepers. He took over Mrs McKilliam's sweet shop at No 17 Union Buildings and opened Hay's Café there. By 1884 he had given up the café and bought the old Newsroom, and in a brilliant stroke, kept the old name. News of his

The fine east-facing frontage of the Athenaeum received only slight damage after the fire of 1973. Something is missing in the foreground. The 'Mannie' has not yet returned from the Green. Centre rear, an unusual view of E&M's. The 'domed' building on the Broad Street corner has gone, but the curtain wall has not yet gone up.

catering expertise spread, and his successor in 1908, John Mitchell, developed the Royal Athenaeum into the famous restaurant that is still recalled by older Aberdonians. Its affectionate sobriquet, 'Jimmy Hay's' not only survived the change in ownership, but endured long after. Following Mitchell's death in 1925, the restaurant was acquired by a consortium of Aberdeen businessmen, which included Andrew Lewis, Isaac Spencer and James Williamson. During their era it reached its zenith as a legendary howff, the café society that Aberdeen never realised it had.

The entrance was from Union Street. From the lobby a stair with a dog-leg turn led up to the first floor, where, in the 1950s, Charlie Middleton, head waiter, held sway at the entrance. The great dining-room, with its simple chandeliers, pilasters and the famous frieze, an imbiber's excuse, that wound round the four walls below the high ceiling of the former Newsroom. 'He that drinks well doth sleep well: He that sleeps well doth think well: He that thinks well doth do well: He that does well drinks well.' A mixed grill was the favoured dish, with deep-fried onions a *specialité de la maison*. Customers would personally select their steaks and watch as they were grilled before their eyes. I can see the chef yet, gloomily (he always looked morose) pocketing the 10/- notes he was slipped at Christmas time. As the meal drew to a close, usually to a sonorous musical accompaniment from the Salvation Army Band down in the Castlegate, Louis the wine waiter would waddle forth with a salver of 'Bennys' from the Athenaeum's amazing stock of liqueurs. At 9.30pm on a Saturday, the younger patrons would make a dash up Broad Street to the Students' Union, which had a late licence, till 10pm.

After these halcyon days, the Athenaeum experienced mixed fortunes. Under the aegis of Thomas Usher & Son Ltd, a revamp took place, including the introduction of trendy continental waiters and the fashionable lowering of the ceiling, with the resulting loss of chandeliers, pilasters and frieze. Such sanitisation marked the end of Jimmy Hay's, and with it a nuance of the 'old' pre-war Aberdeen that had lingered on.

Disaster came on the night of 13 August 1973 when the Athenaeum went up in flames. In the years that followed, total demolition became an option, even though the building was Category A-listed. Fortunately Corner House Hotels Ltd eventually bought the site from Lorimers (formerly Ushers) in November 1977. Planning permission was granted to develop the Athenaeum site for office accommodation, with bars on the ground floor. Two floors of offices have replaced the dining room. But it is not what it was. In retrospect, it would have made an excellent 'overflow' court house, retaining the great dining room as the main courtroom.

The Athenaeum today *from the Union Buildings side.*

From the Shiprow to Market Street

Nos 23–67, the terrace of buildings across the Shiprow gap from the Athenaeum, stretching to the future Market Street, is one of the earliest in Union Street. It was close to the old places of the town, and its familiarity encouraged development. Today that terrace is not intact but many of the original buildings remain. Numbering resumed from the Athenaeum. Nos 23–31 and its neighbour, Nos 33–7, were typical. Both were of four storeys and attic, in smooth granite ashlar like the Athenaeum. No 23 on the Shiprow corner, now the city's Tourist Information Office, had a long tradition of housing clothiers. The family firm of John Falconer, haberdashers, had been there since the early days and George Falconer, who was running the firm by the 1860s, was highly ambitious. So too were Messrs Pratt & Keith, silk mercers at Nos 51–3 (now Alliance & Leicester). Both firms went on to greater things.

In the 1860s, no fewer than twelve members of the clothing trade had businesses here, including a milliner, a staymaker and a mourning establishment which sold widows' weeds and other black garments essential for the bereaved. Many of the shoe shops in this stretch were becoming household names by the late nineteenth century, among them Milne & Munro at No 31 (now the British Heart Foundation), Tylers, later, at No 37 (Costcutter) and Stead and Simpson at No 49 (Semi Chem).

Around 1900, Milne & Munro moved to No 263, where they remained till modern times, and where their golden boot is still to be seen. They were replaced at No 31 by the Maypole, a popular grocery chain of Midlands origin. The Maypole specialised in margarine, as well as eggs, tea, condensed milk and butter. A little further along was another famous 'chain' grocery, Thomas Lipton, 'ham and butter merchant', which by 1883 had opened at No 55, one of the firm's 300 shops. Sir Tommy Lipton, a self-made Glasgow millionaire, was an indefatigable but unsuccessful seeker after the America's Cup yachting trophy, and a great publicist. He cornered the tea market, and many an Aberdeen tram bore the modest slogan 'Liptons – the finest tea the world can produce', the word 'Liptons' being larger than the tram's destination board. Like the Maypole, Liptons was aimed at the mass market, but even so, both shops had stylish, easily recognisable shopfittings. H Samuel, the jewellery chain, had replaced Liptons by the late 1920s. Their clock is still there, a familiar landmark, though Greggs the bakers now sits below it. At the Shiprow end, Mitchell & Muil, Aberdeen's first 'big time' bakers were at No 25 by 1890, complete with tearoom and oval medallions proclaiming their wares. A respectable group of lawyers and accountants were based in the offices above, among them J & G Collie, advocates, handily sited for the sheriff courthouse opposite. David Wyllie opened his bookshop at No 43 in 1814.

The Mitchell & Muil to Market Street stretch in 1946. *Winston Churchill has just been granted the Freedom of the City at the Music Hall and his procession now heads for Marischal College where he will receive the LLD of Aberdeen University. Extreme left, shop assistants stand in the window of Mitchell & Muil, bakers, to see him pass. Right, next but one, the Maypole, and next but one again, the boarded-up shop which will presently provide the Union Street entrance for the new Regal cinema. Right again, note the polychrome detail of the Gibbs surrounds of the first floor windows of Crown Mansions.*

The Regal cinema. *Planned since before the war, the Regal's Union Street entrance opened in 1954. The Maypole is to the left, with the long-established travel agency Mackay Bros above. The cinema's main bulk lay tucked in behind the top of the Shiprow, and it wasn't the first in this area. The Gaiety cinema had been on the Shiprow site since 1908, renamed the Palladium in 1919. By the time it was acquired by the ABC chain in 1937 it was the (not so) New Palladium. Unlike its predecessors, the Regal had a Union Street entrance – ABC had bought a shop to demolish for this purpose. The Regal was renamed the ABC in 1974 and in 1987, it was renamed the Cannon, having become part of that group.*

A narrow pend, No 41½, took one into Crown Court, a T-shaped cul-de-sac containing a hotch potch of buildings. By 1903, Crown Court had been replaced by a magnificent skyscraper, Crown Mansions, built speculatively to provide office space. R G Wilson was the architect. 'Although the venture is a daring one,' pronounced *The People's Guide to Aberdeen*, 'it is believed that the progress and development of Aberdeen in such a marked degree fully justified the expenditure on this singular, stately and handsome pile.'

Crown Mansions could house forty or more tenants on five floors. They were a varied bunch, among them the Medical Officer of Health, council departments, solicitors and chartered accountants, commercial travellers, offices of the North of Scotland College of Agriculture, numerous insurance companies, the Marmite Food Extract Company, a stained glass workshop, hairdressers, the Public Analyst, the Scottish Board of Health, the Old Age Pensions Office and the Scottish Wireless College. The interior was vast and gloomy, with a lift that clanked up and down.

There was a serious fire in 1998, and later a tragic collapse of three floors. After much deliberation about its future, the building was up again by 2004. No 41, the ground floor, is reserved for voluntary associations. No 43, the upper floors, is used for housing association flats. This is a very worthwhile use, but it is disappointing that the entrance of this splendid building should exude a welfare-state dinginess.

*Left, **Crown Mansions restored** after the fire of 1998, and right, its opposite number across Union Street, the former E&M's gents, department. Both were designed by R G Wilson in the late nineteenth-early twentieth centuries.*

Two buildings along from Crown Mansions is the Adelphi, where an arched pend gives access to this court, dating from around 1810. The name derives from the London street designed by the Adam brothers, Adelphi being Greek for brother. This gave Aberdeen an Athenaeum (where philosophers met in ancient times) and an Adelphi within spitting distance of each other – what learned refinement! Inside the pend, however, a genuine new street rather than a court materialises, laid out on the level ground where St Catherine's Hill had supposedly been topped at the very start of the construction of Union Street. But the hill was reluctant to go. As late as 17 November 1813, an advertisement in the *Aberdeen Journal* announced:

> That part of St Catherine's Hill on the east side of the Adelphi removed. Mostly composed of fine sand suitable for building. Sold at 3d halfpenny a load, collected.

The Adelphi has had a mixed fate, but by the end of the twentieth century it was attractively restored with a selection of restaurants, small businesses, a handsome tenement and of course, the Trades Club. It is not a cul-de-sac, but will take you through to the Maritime Museum or on to the Shiprow.

The Royal Hotel and Falconers/Frasers

The city's mail and coach offices were located near the Market Street end, and next door was the coaching inn, the Royal Hotel. During the earlier part of the nineteenth century, hotel and coaches were owned by post horse master Isaac Machray, and from 1855 by his successor David Robertson, well-known characters both. In the *Aberdeen Pub Companion* (1975), Archibald Hopkin has recreated the scene:

> The starting and arrival of the coaches was always an attraction in those pre-railways days and the street outside the Royal used to be astir, as the Union, the Defiance and the Duke of Richmond with their snorting four-in-hand greys set off with their complement of passengers.

On summer evenings the Militia Band used to march back and forward between the Royal Hotel and the Castlegate. Substantial stabling was to the rear, accessed from Putachieside, and by the 1840s, from Market Street. Though the latter was a purely a coaching terminus, it became so deeply ingrained in the Aberdeen mind as a terminus that it survived as such, though in name only, long after the coaches were superseded. Destination boards for the

Woodside tram route used to state 'Market Street–Fountain' or 'Market Street–Woodside' even though there never had been trams or tramlines at the top of Market Street. The Woodside trams began and ended their journeys on the other side of Union Street at St Nicholas Street.

The Royal Hotel, *Aberdeen's most famous coaching inn before it became Falconers.*

Presents or Souvenirs.

FANCY GOODS. BRASS GOODS. LEATHER GOODS
GLOVES, BELTS, HANDKERCHIEFS, SCARFS,
TIES. BLOUSES, UMBRELLAS, SHAWLS.

An early photograph of Falconers, used in the company's adverts. It still retains a hint of the Royal Hotel. The attractive dormer windows, linked by a balustrade, were designed in 1897 by the architect William Kelly.

The Royal was not salubrious. The judge, Lord Cockburn, wrote of his last sitting in Aberdeen in 1853, 'We had a beastly Circuit dinner, on a *sanded floor* [his italics] and came away eagerly this morning from the stinking Royal Hotel …' By this time, another kenspeckle figure, Thomas Douglas, former head waiter at the Royal, was developing the nearby North of Scotland Coffee House into the hotel that would bear his name. At the top of Market Street where it meets Union Street, arcades were built. On the east side, they incorporated a house with a draper's and hatter's on the ground floor.

Around 1870, the draper George Falconer, successor to his uncle John, the founder of the firm, acquired the Royal Hotel to convert into a shop. The Falconers had owned shops in the area since 1788, first in Narrow Wynd, later at No 23 Union Street, but the acquisition of the coaching inn was a gigantic undertaking. George retained the 'Royal' name for years, dubbing his premises at various times, 'Falconer's Royal Galleries', 'Royal Buildings' and 'Royal Arcade'. Falconers' address was now No 65 Union Street, while at No 67 was a dignified new building for National Bank of Scotland. The east side arcades were demolished at this time.

A popular rendezvous for shoppers in Aberdeen and the north-east, Falconers was acquired by the House of Fraser in 1952, and duly re-christened Frasers. In the 1980s, the building underwent a major facelift, its new façade echoing the arcading that had been a feature of the area. Frasers had acquired the neighbouring National Bank of Scotland for demolition but were persuaded by conservation societies to incorporate it instead. The project went £1 million over its £7 million budget, but the firm was determined to refurbish Frasers, Aberdeen, 'as one of the finest Departmental Stores in Europe'. This dream was not quite realised and Frasers closed in 2002. The themed arcading of the frontage, on which so much effort and money was spent, was subsequently fragmented by new arrivals. Falconers/Frasers is missed. With its departure and that of E&M's, there is, unfortunately little to draw one to this stretch of Union Street.

We have now reached Market Street and can retrace our steps to the Castlegate to look at the Town House side.

Falconers in 1975, and a change in window-dressing styles.

Falconers as Frasers. *The 1980s design for 'one of the finest Departmental Stores in Europe'. The former National Commercial Bank on the corner has been neatly incorporated into the scheme.*

Aberdeen FC parade the
European Cup Winners' Cup
*in May 1983. The victory parade
is en route to the Town House,
whose balcony can be seen at the
right. Left of centre at the top of
the picture, the newly cleaned
'Regal' building makes a striking
contrast with Crown Mansions
to its right.*

The North Side: From the Town House to St Nicholas Street

MUNICIPAL BUILDINGS. ABERDEEN. 531A G.W.W.

The Castlegate soon after 1872, when the new Town House was completed. The Castlegate frontage of the Athenaeum is at the left. Right of centre, the tall house with the curved end across the (invisible) Broad Street divide next to the Town House tower was Nos 20–4 Union Street, the start of a fine new terrace dating from 1820–35, perhaps earlier. It became E&M's first Union Street store.

The Esslemont & Macintosh Saga

Esslemont & Macintosh's department store (E&M's to all) now enters the scene. Though Aberdeen had many clothiers in the nineteenth century, none were more ambitious than the Broad Street drapers, Peter Esslemont and William Macintosh. In 1873 they went into partnership as Esslemont & Macintosh, Wholesale and Retail Warehousemen, Drapers and Silk Mercers, based at Macintosh's premises, No 13 Broad Street. Both partners were public men. Esslemont, one of Aberdeen's most able Lord Provosts, held that office from 1880 until 1882, while Macintosh served as a Kincardine county councillor. Before the 1880s were out, E&M's were colonising the west side of Broad Street from Nos 1–13, and by 1894 they had also achieved the great prize, a Union Street frontage, adding the elegant Nos 20–4 to their

The former E&M's 'domed' building, Nos 20–4, after it was acquired by Aberdeen Town Council. The Ladies' Department, Nos 26–30, the former Free Press *building, is on the left.*

properties. The architects Alexander 'Holy' Ellis and R G Wilson gave it an elaborate makeover with a modern shop frontage and an additional fifth floor, complete with dome. This was the firm's main building for years. Cover over the top storey and the original plain building re-emerges. William Macintosh died in 1913. None of his family wished to enter the business, so the store continued with the Esslemonts at the helm for the rest of its independent existence.

After the First World War, E&M's started to progress up Union Street. In 1887 Ellis & Wilson had designed one of the most handsome buildings in Aberdeen for the *Daily Free Press* newspaper, replacing one of the original buildings. Restrained yet ornate, with embellished window surrounds and a row of patera (stone rosettes) below the cornice, the Free Press building, Nos 26-30, formed an island block just west of E&M's corner building. On the ground floor was John Dunn's Globe Boot and Shoe Warehouse but most of the space was given over to the printing and publishing premises of the newspaper. In 1922 the *Daily Free Press* and the *Aberdeen Journal* amalgamated to become the *Press & Journal*. In a move largely dictated by economy, the *Free Press* moved round to the *Journal's* more humble Broad Street office and E&M's stepped in to buy the magnificent *Free Press* building, just across Union Lane from their domed building, Nos 20–4.

With the acquisition of the old *Free Press* building, E&M's had a new neighbour on the other side of St Catherine's Wynd. Sangster & Henderson, at Nos 32–8, was one of the largest firms of drapers and house furnishers in the North-East. By 1897, they had commissioned the architect, R G Wilson, to design a new building studded with oriel windows, replacing one of the originals. He would, in a few years, balance it up with his not dissimilar Crown Mansions on the other side of Union Street.

By 1926 Sangster & Henderson were out of business, scarcely thirty years after their move. Perhaps they had overreached themselves. Aberdeen Town Council stepped in, bought the premises, then negotiated a deal with E&M's. The council would swap the former Sangster & Henderson building for E&M's domed corner building, and much of their Broad Street property as well. Plans to widen Broad Street had already been laid, and when the time was ripe, the demolition of these former E&M's properties could be implemented by the town without the hassle of compulsory purchase. Meanwhile E&M's consolidated its two buildings, one on either side of St Catherine's Wynd. The old *Free Press* building housed three floors of ladies' fashions and a popular restaurant. The gents' department was located at the old Sangster & Henderson building from an early date, and when E&M's wholesale department was phased out, the upper floors were devoted to furnishings.

The Free Press building *became the Ladies' department. It is shown here after E&M's closure.*

The elephants of Billy Smart's Circus *parade down Union Street in 1966. Behind them from right, the lower floors of E&M's former 'domed' building, now in the municipal ownership, housing the city's publicity office as well as a gas showoom and the Singer Sewing Machine shop. Then comes Union Lane, E&M's ladies' department, St Catherine's Wynd and the gents' department. Beyond are Archibald Simpson's early buildings, the former Auchintoul's Mansion, the former Millet's building, and extreme left, Union Chambers, with chimney pots still intact.*

It is 1973. *The 'domed' building has been demolished and little Union Lane has vanished without trace, allowing E&M's to build an ugly concrete curtain wall at the new Broad Street corner. St Nicholas House, earmarked for demolition at time of writing, looms above, right.*

E&M's continued to keep abreast of change, with a hairdressing salon, a wedding boutique, a beauty parlour and a gifts department. A canopy was added, perhaps unnecessarily, to modernise the frontage, and a bridge was built over St Catherine's Wynd, linking the two buildings. The staff, which was eventually managed by five generations of Esslemonts, included the near-immortal Harold, a familiar, bowler-hatted figure, walking down Union Street to work every morning, the elegant Birnie, and the enterprising Norman, who later departed to set up his own business. E&M's remained a privately owned island in a sea of multinationals, witnessing the demise of Isaac Benzie, Watt & Grant, Watt & Milne, Falconers/Frasers and even the mighty Northern Co-op.

In spite of the firm's endeavours, rumours of closure had circulated in Aberdeen for years. By 2005, the writing began to appear on the wall in earnest, when E&M's was purchased by Owen Owen, a Liverpool-based operator of department stores with a somewhat chequered history. Early in 2007, Owen Owen went into administration and E&M's closed that May when no buyer could be found. The closing-down sale was a melancholy affair, as the goods on offer were lumped together in ever-diminishing areas, and customers could wander at will through great empty stretches of the shop floors. At time of writing, there are plans to convert the buildings into a hotel.

Simpson's Debut

We have arrived at Archibald Simpson's first two buildings in Union Street. The first sits next door to Nos 32–6, the former E&M's Gents' department. Simpson was perhaps Union Street's greatest architect. As a young man, he worked in the London office of David Laing, a surveyor to the Customs House and an acquaintance of one of his Dauney uncles, his mother's brothers. 'The first thing I got to do [in Laing's London office] was to make a drawing of Morrison of Auchintoul's house in Union Street,' he wrote to his brother, Sandy. This was a curious coincidence, for Simpson had already made some sketches off his own bat, but had assumed it was too late to submit them (someone, erroneously as it transpired, had told him 'it was half up'). Auchintoul's was a contender to be the earliest house in the new street, and must have been a talking point among architects for months earlier.

Simpson was sent along to Morrison's London house with Laing's own drawings, but Auchintoul was not impressed. Simpson then produced his own sketch, which he happened have with him, and this gained the laird's approval. He then 'worked it up' in Laing's office, and was annoyed that Laing scarcely glanced at his plans yet 'will be paid his thirty or forty guineas and I get nothing for fagging, racing up and down three or four times a day between Laing's office in Bloomsbury and Grosvenor Square', where, presumably, Auchintoul lived. It may not have occurred to our young architect that Laing was irked by such opportunism.

Simpson subsequently left London to study architecture in Rome and Florence, before returning to Aberdeen to complete Morrison of Auchintoul's building. It was advertised to let in the *Aberdeen Journal* of 2 March 1813 as 'that large and elegant house on the north side of Union Street, the property of John Morrison'. It had a suite of public rooms, sculleries, pantries, servants' hall, 'servants' apartments in the roof', numerous closets and extensive cellars in the basement.

Auchintoul's Town House, Nos 40–2, now occupied by Optical Express and other businesses. E&M's former gents' department is just appearing, extreme right.

This building, Nos 40–2, became the Town & County Bank's first home, and was remodelled for the Bank of Scotland in the 1860s. It is difficult to know exactly what Simpson's original building looked like. Today, its most striking feature is the three long windows with pilasters between them, almost reaching the ground floor, a type of façade favoured by bankers. The building is defined by two powerful if neglected entrances, flanked by rusticated stonework, miniature Corinthian columns, and consoles supporting 'balconettes' topped by ball finials. They look too kitsch to be Simpson, but see what you think. The building is now occupied by Optical Express among others. It looks rather frail, but still has dignity. At a later date, the architect James Souttar had offices at No 42, from which he could admire his masterpiece, the Salvation Army Citadel.

A little earlier in that same year of 1813, Simpson had built his first house in Union Street, possibly *the* first in Union Street, 'Auchintoul's Hall'. This was at Nos 46–50, next door but one to Auchintoul's Town House. His clients have been variously cited as the Duchess of Gordon (by W. Douglas Simpson among others) and as John Morrison of Auchintoul (by G. M. Fraser, etc.). If the latter is correct, it is curious that Auchintoul should instruct two such different buildings with only a small gap between them. But in *Aberdeen Fifty Years Ago* (1868), James Rettie, writing from first hand knowledge, states:

Union Chambers, formerly Auchintoul's Hall, at Nos 46–50 Union Street, with the former Millets building to the right.

> On the north side … Mr Morrison of Auchintoul built two large houses, – the one is now the Bank of Scotland's Office, [Nos 40–2], the other next to it, 'Auchintoul's Hall' is now a place of amusement or Music Hall.

Robert Anderson repeats this information in his *Aberdeen in Bygone Days* (1910), adding that, 'Auchintoul's Hall ultimately became the Song School and was transformed into offices a number of years ago'. Auchintoul's Hall was an elegant building with a parapet at roof level and five tall first-floor windows. On the ground floor was a row of arcade-style shop windows and entrances. The most westerly, McCombie's Court, was a genuine walk-through arcade. It gave access to the Netherkirkgate at its junction with Carnegie's Brae, constructed for the convenience of Baillie Thomas McCombie, who had a house built there in 1814.

In the 1900s the building was gutted and reconstructed by the architect James Henderson. It became Union Chambers, 'chambers' indicating offices of a superior type, with the usual ground-floor shops. It was Henderson who added the distinctive wallhead chimneys whose pots survived intact into the 1970s. The original arcading is gone, apart from McCombie's Court, which is convenient for Marks & Spencer's Netherkirkgate entrance.

A curious gap between Auchintoul's two large buildings was filled by the slimline, two-windows-wide No 44, matching the height of its two neighbours, but as narrow as a campanile. For many years from the 1860s, the ground-floor shop was occupied by James Gordon's Mourning Warehouse. Gordon was succeeded by George Bowman, also a mourning specialist, but Bowman also offered the usual ladies' fashions, including 'superb millinery'. By 1922 Millets, out-of-doors specialists, had taken over the premises, though the tent did not straightway replace the tomb, for Millets initially specialised in motoring apparel. An elderly aunt of mine always referred to Millets as 'Bowmans', which I never could understand as a child.

Next to Union Chambers are two rather plain original buildings, dating from around 1820, Nos 52–4 and 56–8. In some prints, Nos 52–4 are shown with a pedimented, covered entrance carried out across the pavement, while its neighbour to the west had a lamp over the door. All this was designed to welcome guests, for both were temperance hotels. No 54 was run by Robert Willock, then the Misses Duffus. It became Benson's Temperance Hotel, then Sutties. No 56 was run by Mrs John Hutcheon. The Central Academy, one of the city's twelve private academies, was also based in this building. Today branches of the Bank of Scotland and Specsavers occupy these premises.

Moving toward St Nicholas Street, the corner building was occupied for many years by Charles Playfair, gunmaker, but he was gone by the early 1860s, dislodged by one of the finest buildings in Union Street. This was Nos 60–2, built in 1863 as the headquarters of the Aberdeen Town and County Bank. Its exterior is a riot of enrichment in pink and grey granite, with lofty pilasters, elegant chimney pots, urns, massive scallops, well-dressed windows, and an arched, pillared entrance with Old Father Time as a keystone. It looks too exotic to be a creation of the architect James Matthews, a town councillor from 1863 to 1871, who looks forth sternly from his photographs. Just as Cincinnatus was recalled from the plough to take charge in Rome as dictator, so James Matthews was recalled from retirement in 1883, to become Lord Provost. While in post, he oversaw the formation of Rosemount Viaduct, only second in importance to the creation of Union Street in its boldness of conception and impact on the development of the city. The former Town and County is now the St Nicholas Street Branch of the Clydesdale Bank. At time of writing there are plans to develop the building as flats.

We have arrived at 'the Queen', though you'll find her today at Queen's Cross.

St Nicholas Street. The Clydesdale Bank, (formerly the Town and County) in its banking days, is on the right, and the Royal Bank of Scotland, formerly the National Commercial, square up across St Nicholas Street with a charmless M & S looking on. The view was out to Powis before the malls blocked the road.

This photograph summarises the territory *covered in this chapter, from the Castlegate to the junctions with St Nicholas Street left, and Market Street, right. Union Chambers rises behind the roof of the tram, chimney pots still intact. Left of Union Chambers are the two temperance hotels, and left again, the magnificent Town and County Bank. Tram No 30 came into service in 1902, Crown Mansions, opposite right, date from 1903 so the photograph is from that era. The driver of RS 290 appears to be offering the Queen a lift. Top hats, boaters and knickerbockers are worn, the fashions are fabulous and a carter is doing a right hand turn into the middle of Union Street. Great days!*

Market Street, looking from Union Street, *as drawn by Archibald Simpson. The arcades, left and right, were a statement about the road's importance, either as the gateway to the harbour or as the grand entrance to Union Street, depending on which way you were going. Next to the east arcade, left, was Simpson's new Post Office of 1842. Across the road is another grand entrance leading into the New Market, the great shopping centre of its day – always 'New', even to the bitter end. Centre right, a horse and cart leaving Hadden Street, part of the scheme, which linked Market Street, the Green and the New Market. It was the meeting place for folk in from the country, and for feeing markets.*

CHAPTER THREE

WESTWARD TO UNION BRIDGE

'I have visited few places where I found warmer friends, or felt myself more at home, than in Aberdeen. The dwellings, being built mostly of granite, remind one of Boston, especially in a walk down Union Street, which is thought to be one of the finest promenades in Europe.'

The American Fugitive in Europe: Sketches of People and Places Abroad,
William Wells Brown, 1855

The South Side: From Market Street to the Back Wynd Stairs to the Green
We reached Market Street in Chapter Two. It had been laid out in 1840–2 by Archibald Simpson in association with his friend and business rival, the city architect, John Smith. It was designed to impress, to remove the wretched hovels of Putachieside, and above all, to provide a route between Union Street and the developing harbour.

Union Street, between Market Street and Union Bridge, did not begin to fill with buildings until post-bankruptcy, that is until after 1824. Before that time this stretch had its hazards. Coorse loons standing on Union Street pitched stones down the chimneys of houses in the Green for sheer devilment, while a low wall had to be built to prevent pedestrians from being blown down onto the Green on windy days. Enterprising Green-dwellers built wooden walkways from their upper storeys to gain access to Union Street, and tradesmen advertised their services on placards affixed to their chimneys. After buildings went up, and particularly after the Market Street scheme boosted development, the south side became a prime shopping area.

Since around 1900, No 73, on the west arcade corner, had been the base of Hay & Lyall, 'carvers and gilders to the Queen, print sellers, opticians and artists' colourmen'. John Hay, founder of the firm, engraved many of the famous old prints of Aberdeen. William Wilson, who cast the leopard finials on Union Bridge, was one of the firm's many talented employees. Their neighbours upstairs at No 75 were Messrs Horne & Mackinnon, part of a small stockbroker colony that developed in the east end of Union Street from its early days.

By the mid-1920s, both firms were gone and Style & Mantle, furriers, were in residence. Not long after, a Montague Burton tailor's shop opened nearby at Nos 81–3. Burton, a

Lithuanian Jewish immigrant originally named Mesche Osinsky, had arrived in Britain a few years earlier, changed his name, and was now doing very well in the tailoring business. By 1929, Montague Burton had replaced Style & Mantle on this corner, and the arcade had been removed, making it, commercially, a very attractive site. Had the determined and successful Burton engineered the move, and the removal of the arcade? Style & Mantle relocated to a somewhat less desirable site beside the Adelphi. Burton's handsome new premises, designed by the architect George Watt, had a touch of art deco. Burton's was later transmogrified into Top Man and Top Shop, part of Philip Green's highly successful Arcadia group.

June 1930. There are no traffic lights at the top of Market Street. The west arcade shown on the right side of Simpson's drawing, page 46, and the Style & Mantle premises were demolished soon after. The shop at the extreme left was later occupied by Knowles fruiterers, who were caught up in these musical chairs and moved here from No 77 Union Street.

The same corner and the Coronation Procession, June 1953. *Crowds flock to Union Street between Market Street and St Nicholas Street to watch. Queen Victoria looks towards the handsome New Market entrance. Burton, on the Style & Mantle site, has not yet become Top Shop. A good vantage point has been secured by the men dangling outside Knowles, fruiterers.*

The same corner. *The Top Shop/Top Man fascia cuts into the Burton building. Left, Knowles is replaced by Na-Na fashions, and left again, the Aberdeen Market entrance that was substituted for the magnificent New Market granite façade.*

Moving from the 'Top Man corner' to Union Street, the various shops in this stretch in the late nineteenth century are mostly forgotten, but they have left us stylish advertisements. Lumsden & Gibson, Italian warehousemen, who survived into modern times, were at No 95 and George Lyall & Co, silk mercers and favourites with the gentry, were at Nos 97–9. Elijah Burwell had his Fancy Bazaar at No 101. 'His toys and other fancy good were of a magnificence quite beyond us,' recalled Lachlan Mackinnon, who did not come from a poor home, in his *Recollections of an Old Lawyer* (1935). R K Smith, hatter and outfitter, took over at No 101 in the 1880s after Burwell's retirement to Ballater.

George Jamieson, 'jeweller to the Queen', trading in Union Street since the 1840s, was at No 107. He had moved to No 125 by 1908, when the business was acquired by W W Carry. W Davidson & Son, 'breeches makers and hosiers', were at No 123. Their advert, complete with illustration, proudly stated, 'Directly opposite the Façade' – John Smith's handsome colonnade which fronted the Kirkyard of St Nicholas.

George Rezin & Son, clothiers, were at No 139, next door to D A Mortimer (later Mortimer & Dunn), chemist, at No 141, which also served as a Post Office. Mortimer regularly advertised his alarming-sounding 'Carbolised Rose Tooth Powder' which 'destroys the unpleasantness arising from decay'. Of the eight shops mentioned here, five were in the clothing business, and there were numerous others of that ilk in the same stretch.

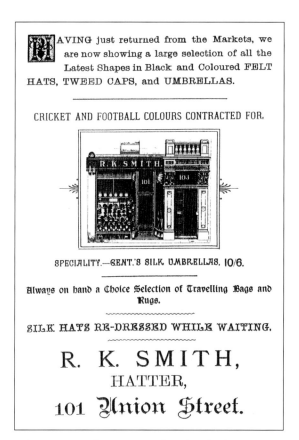

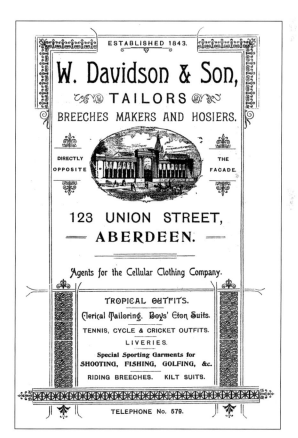

Advertisement for R K Smith. *Like all advertisers at this time, Smith was at considerable pains to emphasise both his street number, and the landmark 'balconette' next door. No 101 later became the Princess Café.*

Nineteenth century tailors *used local landmarks to help promote their wares. R K Smith incorporated a drawing of the ornate doorway at No 103, and W Davidson & Son the façade fronting St Nicholas graveyard opposite.*

A dreich day in 1957 *and another view of the National Bank of Scotland, left, before it was absorbed by Frasers. West of Burton is Strathdee the baker and Paige's dress shop. Partly covered by the umbrella are the rusticated arches of No 93 Union Street, a fine Archibald Simpson building and at this time offices of the North British and Mercantile Insurance Co. It began life as a Town and County Bank. Beyond is the broad fascia of Grants, house furnishers, (now Internaçionale) with the entrance to the New Market and the Princess Café disappearing into the distance.*

THE
SCOTTISH PROVINCIAL ASSURANCE COMPANY.
(ESTABLISHED 1825.)
INCORPORATED BY SPECIAL ACT OF PARLIAMENT.

Above, an advertisement for the Scottish Provincial Assurance Company showing Simpson's building at No 93, with distinctive rusticated arcading, the same building as shown opposite but at an earlier period. It had started life as the Town and County Bank, with the long arched windows favoured by bankers. No address was necessary, so well known was the building. Below, after the Aberdeen Markets/BhS development it was demolished and replaced by this ugly frontage.

The New Market

The New Market of 1842 was a superb hall on three levels, designed by Simpson for the sale of local produce. It could be entered from the grand entrance in Market Street, but the popular entrance was on Union Street between Nos 95–9 and Nos 101–5, gaunt buildings of 1825 'in the style of Simpson'. These run from the Internaçionale store, at time of writing, to the railing of the Green 'gap', which looks down to where Correction Wynd, arched over by Union Street, emerges onto the Green.

The former entrance to the New Market (and the present Aberdeen Market), is at the middle of this 'style of Simpson' block of two buildings, left. 'Office' is currently a shoe shop on the old Princess Café site, which earlier still was R K Smith's tailor's shop at No 101. 'Office' is entered below the ornate little balcony seen in R K Smith's advert. The shop to the right was once A C Little. The railing, centre, gives a view of the Green below.

Shopping in the New Market in 1964.

The New Market's Union Street entrance, as shabby as the Market Street entrance was grand, took the shopper out over the East Green and so into the New Market at the rear end. It may have been a later addition, created after Simpson's death, to save customers the haul round to Market Street, for I doubt if Simpson would have tolerated such an undistinguished corridor between his two (putative) buildings, and at least would have given it an arcade.

A tragic fire in April 1882 devastated the first New Market, leaving only its walls standing, but it was quickly rebuilt in a more homely style, and if anything its popularity increased. It was classless and timeless, selling wholesome local produce. All the well known butchers had shops there. Spence Alsop vied with John Williamson, John Laidlaw, James Sangster and James McIntosh with displays of sides of beef, poultry and game, rabbits, sausages, liver, pigs' trotters, sheeps' heads, cartons of jellied chicken and potted heid. There was an indefinable smell, boosted by odours from the noisy and cheerful People's Café, by newly boiled beetroot and freshly made market candy. There were fruit and vegetable stalls, and the Ellon Stall with its butter, oatcakes, eggs, honey and home-made crowdie. Down the steep granite stairs was the cool basement with its marble slabs, the realm of the fish stalls where several of the fishmongers were royal warrant holders.

Redevelopment, involving British Home Stores (now BhS), brought about the closure of New Market on 6 January 1971. It was speedily taken down in the face of widespread protest. Many older Aberdonians still cannot come to terms with its uncalled-for demise and the historian Dr Alexander Keith wrote of how it had 'succumbed to the vandalism of Big Business as licensed by the Town Council'. The loss of the unique Market Street entrance was totally unacceptable.

The replacement shopping centre bore no comparison. A fine building at No 93, shown on page 53 and designed by Simpson in 1826 as the first headquarters for the Town & County Bank, also went. After the Bank moved to the St Nicholas Street corner in 1860, this building was occupied by the Scottish Provincial Assurance Company, then from about 1900 until the end by the North British and Mercantile Insurance Co. Such was the anger and concern surrounding the destruction of the New Market that the demolition of No 93 to make way for the British Home Stores shop went ahead with little protest.

Further west R K Smith moved from No 101 to Nos 113-119. Woolworths took over the latter premises in the early 1920s, while R K Smith's caravan finally rested at No 403, remaining in business for another decade. The Woolworths site is easy to identify, not merely because it is now a McDonald's, but also by its curiously disembodied first-floor fenestration at No 119 perhaps originally inserted at R K Smith's instigation. There are three arched windows and a pup, all with Gibbs surrounds and pilasters. At some point these may have continued to the ground floor, giving the building an air of grandeur, before they were truncated at a later date by the insertion of the plate-glass shop front.

Woollies had stairs on either side of its ground floor, taking one up to the first floor which sold everything from gym shoes to kirby grips. Central stairs on the ground floor led down to the lower ground floor where household goods and a reasonable food counter were located. A back stair, descending a further storey, gave access to the Green and one could criss-cross between Boots, Woolworths and the New Market, using their back entrances.

The hub of Union Street shopping in 1959 with Woolworths taking centre stage Extreme left, No 105, beside the Green 'gap' was the dress shop, set up by Mr A C Little in the 1920s, offering 'something to wear that is well cut smart and practical and not too expensive'. It was still there in the 1980s. After the gap and True-Form Shoes and Woolworths came the Home & Colonial, with awning at No 121, famed for its dairy produce. The assistants wore waitress-style caps and skilfully worked chunks of butter to the required weight between two butter pats. Another favourite, extreme right, was No 123, the Scotch Wool and Hosiery Stores, later the Scotch Wool Shop.

After the departure of Woolworths, *the arrival of McDonald's, the 'hamburger giants' was not without controversy. 'Fast footwork and a slick deal to bring Big Mac to Union Street,' was how the local press summed up the planning committee's handling of the application in October 1990. 'Fast food takeaways are not the way to arrest the decline in Union Street's image and prestige,' pronounced a local MP. Indicating, perhaps, that they were as worthy of Union Street as Woolworths, McDonald's gave the building a £1.7 million overhaul, making a feature of the quirky windows and cleverly attempting to continue the line of the pilasters to pavement level to reprise the original effect.*

Boots in 1973.

Woolworths was not the first of Union Street's big chain stores. Boots the Chemists came to Aberdeen just before the First World War, and moved in at No 141, recently vacated by Mortimer & Dunn, chemists, then expanded in the mid-1920s, moving the short distance down to Nos 133–9½, the building immediately west of the Back Wynd Stairs. By 1932 the dangerous old 'Jacob's Ladder', dating from the laying out of Union Street, was replaced by modern stairs whose balustrades bear a Greek key motif. Boots upgraded its building in 1936 in art deco style, designed by George Bennett Mitchell & Son, architects.

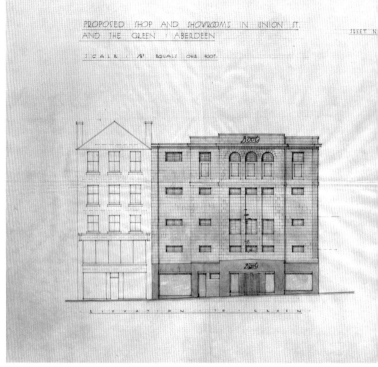

Left. **Before Union Street was built** *Back Wynd linked St Nicholas Kirk with the Green via the steep Aedie's Brae, which was, in effect, the lower half of Back Wynd. After Union Street cut across the Wynd, the Stairs replaced the steep brae. This explains why Back Wynd is on one side of the street and the Stairs on the other. The original Back Wynd Stairs, left, were more of a Jacob's Ladder and possibly even less user-friendly than Aedie's Brae. To the right is the side of No 131, where the great physicist, James Clerk Maxwell, once had rooms. To the left is a rare view of a 'blind' arch under Union Street, beside the 'cartie, and the rear of Boots. The Queen's Cinema and James Allan furniture shop are on the other side of Union Street.*

Right: George Bennett Mitchell's drawing for the new rear elevation of Boots, viewed from the Green.

The current Back Wynd Stairs, *which replaced the Jacob's Ladder in 1932. They illustrate just how high Union Street was built above the Green. The small parking area, right, was the site of Aedie's House. In the mid-eighteenth century it played a disreputable role in the slave trade. Unwary young lads, playing around the harbour area, were kidnapped, sold to plantation owners and imprisoned here until a slave-ship arrived to transport them to the Americas. Only one boy, Peter Williamson, eventually returned and unmasked the ringleaders of this lucrative business – none other than the city's magistrates and leading officials.*

Boots was an interesting place to shop. The dispensing counter at the back of the ground floor was always crowded, and in those days there was a vet's section, selling products much more interesting than human potions. The escalator, when it was working, took one down to the gift department and lending library on the lower floor, where doors gave access to the Back Wynd Stairs at the halfway landing, easing the descent to the Green. Down at the Green level, Boots' goods entrance was also given a simple and attractive art deco makeover.

Like Woolworths, this, the main branch of Boots, moved to the Bon Accord Centre which was opened by the Queen in 1990. Her Majesty took the opportunity to express concern about the fate of Union Street. The former Boots shop became Virgin Megastores, then Zavvi. Today the doors leading to the Back Wynd Stairs are locked and the rear entrance has a neglected air.

When coming up the Back Wynd Stairs to Union Street, look out for an exceptionally modest little plaque at the top right-hand side, which states that James Clerk Maxwell, the eminent physicist 'lived in this house from 1856 to 1860'. (Its location is officially given as No 131 Union Street).

'This house', No 131, turns out to be Thorntons chocolates, and it was also a shop in Clerk Maxwell's time. He possibly lodged at No 129 – upstairs at the same building, now a dentist's. Albert Einstein found Clerk Maxwell's work 'the most profound and most fruitful that physics has experienced since the time of Newton', and hereby hangs a sad tale, at least for Aberdeen. When King's and Marischal Colleges amalgamated in 1860, the problem of two professors for each chair arose. It was agreed that the senior professor should retire on full salary. In one case only, because of University politics, the older, King's College, professor stayed, while Clerk Maxwell, the Marischal man had to leave, 'and so the University of Aberdeen lost the greatest scientist who ever graced her walls,' commented Professor R. V. Jones.

Nos 123–31 housed other well-remembered shops, including Salisbury the handbag shop at No 127 and, up near Union Bridge, Saxone's shoe shop at No 141.

Where the Back Wynd Stairs meet Union Street. *The plaque to James Clerk Maxwell is scarcely visible to the naked eye. Boots has become Zavvi.*

The North Side: From St Nicholas Street to Belmont Street

The Peterkins (ex-Gloucester Hotel) Terrace

We now cross to the north side, to the terrace which runs from St Nicholas Street to the Correction Wynd Stairs, beside the colonnade at St Nicholas Kirkyard, originally from No 72 to No 106. When this row was built around 1820, it curved at both ends. By the mid-1850s there was a mixture of shops on the ground floor, with Angus Fraser the grocer at No 72 and

This late nineteenth-century photograph reveals many of the buildings to be investigated in this section. From left, Back Wynd, and a glimpse of St Nicholas Kirkyard, with the splendid mausoleum of Dr Robert Hamilton of Hamilton Place fame, far left. The Kirkyard is fronted by John Smith's fine colonnade, and right, beyond the Correction Wynd Stairs (not visible) is the former Gloucester Hotel block, much of which is now occupied by the legal firm of Peterkins. It is one of Union Street's earliest buildings, much of it erected before 1824 and thought by some to be by Archibald Simpson. Its curving ends are still intact. The darker building beyond the St Nicholas Street gap, is the Town and County Bank of 1863, (now the Clydesdale), discussed in Chapter Two.

John Kay, druggist, at No 74. That was before he went into partnership with Charles Davidson. Also in residence there was James Cassie RSA, the well known portrait and landscape painter, who 'gypsied' his way from lodging to lodging up and down Union Street. Cassie once attended a dinner at which Edinburgh and Glasgow academicians were extolling the merits of their respective birthplaces as the true cradle of Scottish art. Eventually Cassie interrupted indignantly: 'De'il a bit! – there's Jameson, Dyce and Philip – tak' awa' Aiberdeen and twal mile roon an' far are ye?' His meaning was clear: if you discount the great Aberdeen painters, Scottish art would have little to offer.

The seedsmen, Cardno & Darling were next door, then David Gill the watchmaker, whose son, later Sir David Gill, the Astronomer Royal, once worked as his assistant. Sir David was credited with some of the earliest photographs of the Moon. George Pegler, fruiterer, another nomad, was at No 80. Charles Playfair, gunmaker, dislodged by the Town & County Bank, was at No 84, James Duffus, confectioner, at No 86, James Berry, another watchmaker, at No 88, Lockhart & Salmond, confectioners, at No 92, and John Watson's Private Hotel was at No 102. All were well known in their day.

Banished to the upper floors were the advocates, dentists, accountants and insurance companies, tailors and dressmakers and lodgers. At the corner shop nearest the kirkyard, at No 106, the versatile William Smith Jnr, tea merchant, also ran the County Fire Office. Within this busy row, and at the New Market just across the road, residents could easily find the needs of a lifetime.

The first major change to the original block came during 1887–8 near the St Nicholas Street end. The Edinburgh-based Commercial Bank of Scotland pulled down Nos 78–80 and erected in their place, a tall, narrow, ecclesiastical-style building, Sydney Mitchell & Wilson, architects. An interesting building in itself, it disrupted the unity of the hitherto immaculate row.

More drastic changes followed. At the end of 1928, the Commercial Bank demolished the ecclesiastical-style building which had stood for only forty years and with it, the curved corner building, dislodging H Samuel jewellers at No 72 and the Singer Sewing Machine Company, which had been there since 1888. In their place, Jenkins & Marr, architects, produced a handsome 'cuboid colossus', with slab-like sides and Corinthian columns. Ionic, the usual order for Union Street, was perhaps not grandiose enough.

The banking institutions of the 'Gloucester' block. *Top right, this terrace from the St Nicholas Street end, with the new Commercial Bank of Scotland of 1887, sticking up like the proverbial sore thumb, or in this case, finger, centre right. The C B Birch statue of Queen Victoria, at the east side of St Nicholas Street, extreme right, replaced a marble version of the young Queen. Top left, the architect's drawing for the new bank. Bottom left, the handsome new Royal Bank of 1928, previously the Commercial Bank of Scotland then the National Commercial. Bottom right, photographed during a snow storm, the door of the RBS, with more acroteria (architectural embellishments shaped like the ace of spades) than you can shake a stick at. Montague Burton across the road only had two.*

Although the curving end was lost, St Nicholas Street was wider at this corner than before. One bank, even a large one, did not take up so much space as the two earlier buildings on this site. In 1959, the National Bank and the Commercial Bank merged to become the National Commercial Bank of Scotland and in 1969, following a further merger, the National Commercial 'cuboid colossus' became a Royal Bank of Scotland branch.

Back at the Correction Wynd Stairs end, by 1860 John Watson's Private Hotel at No 102 had become the grim-sounding 'Temperance Hotel, William Forsyth, keeper', and began a steady eastward advance. The Misses Walker were the proprietors of the Forsyth Temperance Hotel in the 1870s until E. Gardiner took over around 1908. His reign was short-lived and the ladies took over again – Miss C Jack, Mrs McDonald and Miss McIver. By 1921, it was simply The Forsyth Hotel. It became The Gloucester in 1950, stressing in its adverts that it was fully licensed. It was a popular, well-frequented city-centre rendezvous for weddings and social functions, for dropping in for a coffee, with a jazz club in the basement, and with famous revolving doors.

Not much lane discipline in this photograph from the 1930s outside the Forsyth Hotel. The No 6a bus served the Duthie Park route, the No 20, Old Aberdeen. The hotel has a 'balconette' of wrought iron above its door, and beyond lay John Smith's colonnade. By the 1940s and fifties, a row of well remembered shops were at street level. Raffan & Sons, menswear, George Dickie, booksellers, Leslie Hatt, hosier, R J Smith, draper Charles Stott, florists, and Finlay & Co tobacconists, succeeding James Yule. These are illustrated on the Contents page.

In the 1980s, the Aberdeen Hotel Company sold the Gloucester to Embassy Hotels, who carried out a much-needed refurbishment. Even so, it closed for good in December 1988, sold to the clothing retail chain, Next who planned to develop the St Nicholas Street, Correction Wynd Union Street, St Nicholas Lane area – 'The Golden Triangle', as it was nicknamed – into yet another multi-million-pound covered shopping mall of which the Gloucester would be a part.

The scheme ran into difficulties. The popular Prince of Wales pub in St Nicholas Lane refused to have anything to do with it. Its proprietor, backed by considerable support, stood firm and there was considerable hostility to the whole project, whatever its merits.

By this time, the neoclassical ambience of central Union Street had been damaged by several inappropriate developments. Aberdonians would tell you they were scunnered by out-of-town speculators and clueless councillors playing fast and loose with the heritage. In 1990, Next announced general losses of over £46 million and no more was heard of The Golden Triangle. The old Gloucester building stood empty for some years, but at the end of 1994 was acquired by the Aberdeen law firm of Peterkins, and now looks as good as new. The majority of the street-level shops sell mobile phones.

The Correction Wynd Stairs in 1979. The Wynd has been arched over by Union Street, in the style approved by the surveyor Abercrombie. The Green 'gap' is between buildings on the other side of Union Street and the Green itself can just be glimpsed under the arch.

A last glimpse of both sides of this section. On the south side, right, A C Little, the Market entrance Princess Café are still there. Grants, house furnishers has not yet become Internaçionale, nor has the Assurance building with the rusticated arches become BhS. On the north side, the Gloucester has taken over most of the block. Raffans Menswear has become Dunn, H Samuel is still there as it was in the early days while the RBS stands square at what was once a round end.

The Gloucester has become Peterkins, the legal firm. Extreme left, railings indicate where Correction Wynd goes under Union Street. John Smith's Colonnade and St Nicholas Kirkyard are just out of sight.

The Colonnade. *In 1820, John Smith designed a magnificent colonnade of Dancing Cairns granite as a memorial to a noted benefactor, Sir John Forbes of Newe. It gave St Nicholas' Kirkyard a grand entrance and at the same time screened it off from Union Street. The central archway is flanked by double Ionic columns with six smaller columns on either side, linked by railings. Out of sight are the massive pylons which anchor the colonnade at each end. (John Smith also built bridges). It is based on London's Hyde Park Screen, built a decade earlier by the English architect, Decimus Burton, who was also involved with the Aberdeen colonnade in its early stages.*

Before the colonnade was built, the graveyard was smaller and unkempt, with wasteland to the south. Here the popular travelling shows came: jugglers, fire-eaters, swings and merry-go-rounds, giants, dwarfs, wild beasts and peep shows. In 1819, such fun and games came to an end. The wasteland between the Correction and Back Wynds, extending forty yards to Union Street, was purchased and added to the kirkyard. Thus Salvation saw off Damnation. Behind the colonnade lies St Nicholas' Kirkyard and the two Kirks of St Nicholas, East and West, successors to the great Mither Kirk, which was divided in two after the Reformation of 1560.

The West Kirk of St Nicholas was designed by the Aberdonian James Gibbs, the architect of St Martin-in-the-Fields in London, the Radcliffe Camera in Oxford, and the Senate House in Cambridge. It replaced the ruinous medieval nave (the people's area) of the Mither Kirk from 1741. The master mason was a Kincardineshire man, James Wylie, so handsome that the girls followed him around Aberdeen.

The creation of the East Kirk, to the right, was the subject of an unseemly row. Its medieval predecessor had been the choir (sacred to the clergy) of the Mither Kirk but this 'was destroyed in the year 1835', as James Rettie recalled in *Aberdeen Fifty Years Ago* (1868).

The culprits were an unlikely a trio of vandals, its minister, the Rev. Dr James Foote, the provost, James Blaikie, and the architect, Archibald Simpson. Apparently Foote had taken umbrage when a colleague, the Rev. John Murray, became minister of John Smith's splendid new North Kirk in King Street. He was determined to have a new church too and Archibald Simpson, who never let conservation stand in his way, saw the opportunity to build a city-centre showpiece. Although the roof of the medieval East Kirk showed signs of decay, it was repairable and the walls were good. Simpson, however, pronounced it unfit for purpose. The formidable trio swept a chorus of protests aside, had it demolished and in 1835 erected the new East Kirk in Dancing Cairns granite.

On the evening of 9 October 1874, the ancient oak steeple of St Nicholas' and Simpson's new East Kirk, which had stood for less than forty years, were burnt down in one of the city's most dramatic fires, when Union Street and the two Wynds were jammed with horrified spectators. Fortunately the East Kirk was quickly and faithfully restored by William Smith, son of John, who was also responsible for the splendid new granite steeple.

Left, St Nicholas Kirkyard showing James Gibbs' West Kirk left, the medieval oak steeple and Drum's Aisle, centre and right, a sight of Simpson's new East Kirk before it was burnt down. Right, a rare photograph of the great fire of 1874 just before the oak steeple crashed onto the ruins of the East Kirk. 'For a few minutes the fiery skeleton was etched against the skyline, then it toppled, menacingly towards Schoolhill'. The West Kirk, left, was relatively unscathed.

In 1980, after years of discussion, the congregations of the East and West Kirks amalgamated as the Kirk of St Nicholas Uniting. At time of writing, the East Kirk is being redeveloped at three levels, with community involvement in mind. In 2006, prior to redevelopment, Aberdeen City Council's Archaeological Unit carried out a major dig in the church and uncovered a wealth of material, including flint tools over 8,000 years old, evidence of an eleventh or twelfth century church, scallop shells indicating a pilgrimage to Santiago de Compostela in Spain, child burials, burials from the fifteenth century church and early graveyards on the site.

The dig at the former East Kirk of St Nicholas, watched from the gallery by members of the public.

Lockhart & Salmond's restaurant in the old Advocates' Hall, with its rusticated, arcade-style ground floor still intact. Below the parapet, three sets of handsome Ionic columns, arranged in pairs, flank tall windows. The building assumed a more modest mien after turning into Back Wynd, with pilasters instead of Ionic pillars, more appropriate for a humble wynd, engaging themselves modestly against the wall.

We have arrived at the junction of Union Street and Back Wynd. John Smith's brilliant corner-turner used to be the Queen's Cinema and that's how many Aberdonians remember it. Smith built it as Advocates' Hall, for the Society of Advocates in Aberdeen. The foundation stone was laid in November 1836 and at the Society's Inaugural Dinner there exactly two years later there were fifty-three toasts, the forty-second of which honoured 'John Smith, the Architect of the Buildings'.

But the lawyers were not entirely epicurean. The Hall apart, the building also contained private chambers, meeting rooms and the splendid first-floor library. George Grub, the librarian, was a prolific scholar, historian and Professor of Law at Aberdeen University. In 1872, the advocates moved to the new Advocates' Hall in Concert Court, Broad Street for convenient access to the new Sheriff Courts. In the following year Lockhart & Salmond, nearby confectioners, bought old Advocates' Hall. They ran a restaurant on the premises until 1882.

The next occupant was the Conservative Club, which undertook ambitious alterations and introduced a curvaceous iron balcony which snaked below the Ionic ensemble as far as the Back Wynd frontage. The Tories stayed only a few years. By the late 1880s, George Watson was running a restaurant at No 118, the ground floor, while the Queen's Rooms –doubtless named in honour of the Golden Jubilee of 1887 – were upstairs at No 120.

This was the first reference to the name that would stick. The building was sold again in 1890 and enjoyed a varied career, becoming over the next few years the Queen's Rooms and Aberdeen Auction Company in 1894–5, the Queen's Billiard Salon, and the Queen's Restaurant from 1899.

At this time, the architect, A Marshall Mackenzie, carried out a number of alterations. In 1909 as the Queen's Buildings, it was bought by another Mackenzie, J R of that name, the Belmont Street auctioneer, to serve as salerooms. Later, J R Mackenzie caught the new movie bug and converted the place into the Queen's Cinema, which opened in 1913 in the domed and handsomely decorated main hall. In 1927, the Queen's was acquired by James F Donald of the famous Aberdeen cinema dynasty.

The Queen's Cinema, 1969.
Over the years it acquired several interesting little windows and cinematic appurtenances, including a vertical neon cinema sign. Another vertical cinema sign may be made out in Back Wynd, right, advertising 'Donald's Opticians' – perhaps testament to the legendary ingenuity of this amazing family. The rusticated stonework below the pilasters, to the left of the opticians', was the frontage of the Conservative Club bar. It later became the Queen's Bar, with a mock baronial theme, and is now Ninety-Nine, a traditional pub. The ground-level shops on Union Street were occupied for decades by M K Gillespie, fruiterers, and later Esson, tobacconists, and Lizars, opticians. The current occupants are Beaverbrook's, jewellers, and Molton Brown.

In June 1936 the cinema caught fire and the interior was completely destroyed. Strengthened and handsomely refurbished with increased seating, it rose from the ashes. The Donalds were generous with their complimentary tickets, and as only second-run films were shown, it was a popular place to catch up with a film missed first time round. The Queen's closed in 1981 for the usual reasons, and after it had stood empty and deteriorating for some years, the Donalds converted it into a nightclub in 1987. It was known as Eagles, then Legends, and is now called Espionage – though that could indicate that it had become a training centre for aspiring spies.

Next door to the Queen's Cinema was the plain, elegant No 122. Here there was not an Ionic column, not a pediment nor a pilaster in sight; only the modest parapet continuing along from the Queen's. The building's only concession to grandeur was the coat-of-arms denoting that James Allan & Son, cabinetmakers, were royal warrant holders. James Allan, initially as Allan & Macallan, had occupied that building since it first went up. In the 1930s the architect and tycoon, Tommy Scott Sutherland, bought the firm for £22,000 and took it successfully through a financially difficult period before selling on. In more recent times, No 122 was occupied by Mothercare, but it has lain empty and neglected since 2005. At one time it was in danger of becoming an amusement arcade.

James Allan & Company, cabinetmakers, at No 122.

Union Bridge and, centre right, the Aberdeen Hotel, soon after 1820. *Between them these landmarks provided a grand entrance to the city. Harry Lumsden of Belhelvie's townhouse, No 1 Union Terrace, is extreme left. The cottages in the foreground, 'red-pantiled hovels' are in Windmill Brae. The tall buildings, Nos 130–2, across the Belmont Street gap from the Aberdeen Hotel were designed by Archibald Simpson, with his office upstairs on the corner. In 1826, these buildings went on fire and precious plans and papers were lost. To the right are a huddle of old buildings beside the entrance to Back Wynd, then St Nicholas' Kirk, with its original oak steeple, to be burned down in the fire of 1874. Smith's colonnade is not yet in place. Right of the steeple, the buttresses of the medieval East Kirk may be glimpsed.*

A close up of the same view in 1974. *The Victoria Restaurant, a popular rendezvous which opened in the mid-fifties, has replaced the Aberdeen Hotel. Jamieson & Carry, jewellers, is below, and in the foreground is a glimpse of the south side of Union Bridge before the shops went up. Right of the bus, just visible, emerging from Belmont Street (traffic on the bridge is single line, and buses have been re-routed) is the tall building which initially included the Archibald Simpson office. It was rebuilt after the fire of 1826, a 'twin' has been added, and the group expanded to the east. This block now numbers Nos 122½-132 and currently includes Symington's/Reed Employment and O'Brians/McColls. Irene Adair Fashions and Munro's Tourist Agency were located here in modern times. Opposite the bus, extreme right are, No 122 James Allan/Mothercare and the former Queen's Cinema.*

CHAPTER FOUR

THE GRAND ARCH

'A gentleman on horseback passed along the line of Union Street and crossed the Grand Arch over the Denburn on his way out of town.'

Aberdeen Journal, 23 September 1805

We are almost at Union Bridge, the Grand Arch, the great jewel in Union Street's crown. The struggle that it took to get it, quite literally, off the ground is told in Chapter One. Now we hardly realise that it's there. The topography of the Bridge differs from that of the Street, so we can abandon the usual south side/north side format, and start just west of Belmont Street, where Chapter Three ended.

The Aberdeen Hotel

Bestriding the west side of Belmont Street and the north-east side of Union Bridge is a great colossus, Nos 134–44. This was built in 1817, the year of Aberdeen's bankruptcy, for the Aberdeen Hotel, under the management of William McGregor, with Archibald Simpson as architect. It was perhaps the building's magnificent bulk which prompted the judge, Lord Medwyn, in Aberdeen to preside over the Northern circuit, to remark: 'it was a city without an entrance; now it is an entrance without a city'. Union Bridge and the Aberdeen Hotel formed the grand entrance (rather than the true, but rather unimpressive entrance, 'the footpath or lane leading from the Damhead Road', i.e. the present Summer Street).

For the front of the Aberdeen Hotel building, Simpson used granite ashlar and bull-faced granite for the lower reaches, making good use of the levels on the Belmont Street and Denburn Road sides, the latter seven storeys, all told. As was to be expected, there were arcade-style windows and doors at ground-floor level on Union Street where there were shops. Simpson used the same style at the same level for the frontages of Belmont Street and Denburn Road. The ground may have gone from under his feet, but he keeps the rhythm. He also indulges his passion for broad panels on top of the parapets, surmounted by neat chimneys, stuck in like candles on a birthday cake, on the building's three frontages.

From the early days, James Littlejohn, a woollen draper and furnisher of gents' apparel had his 'fancy worsted warehouse' at Nos 134–6, on the ground floor of the Aberdeen Hotel building, with ample room for workshops on the floors below. John Ford of the Royal Glass and China Galleries, Edinburgh, moved into No 136, when Littlejohn crossed the road in 1848. By 1875, Ford had expanded to take over No 138, and in 1901 Stoke-born Joseph William Baker, a time-served apprentice with Coalport arrived to manage the business. Ford must have been a fair age by this time, and three years later Baker took over and ran the firm as J W Baker Ltd. It was in this era that Baker's began to produce commemorative plates. Their first venture, the Marischal College Plate of 1907, to celebrate the brilliant new façade, is a collector's piece.

J W Baker's frontage, 1974. The shop's handsome façade, with leaded glasswork, neat pilasters and eighteenth-century-style ceramic insets sets the tone for the quality of goods inside.

J W Baker died in 1941 and his son Jack took over. He was in turn succeeded by his nephew, Manchester-born John Whitehead, who became managing director in 1971. His annual visits to the Stoke potteries kept him in touch with developments within the industry and Baker's stock now included a wide range of fine china, figurines, glass and earthenware by all the leading manufacturers. Here was a local shop that was specialist enough to sell to a worldwide clientele.

On John Whitehead's retirement, Baker's was acquired by another local firm, but this venture was not successful and Baker's closed in 2004, a sad loss to Union Street. Fopp, a music chain moved into the property, but called in the receivers in 2007. At time of writing, the occupants are All Saints Fashion Clothing.

Back upstairs, the Aberdeen Hotel closed in 1858 and soon afterwards large wooden boards affixed to the monumental west side announced the presence of John Fraser, Auctioneer and Valuator on the second and third floors, with Charles Playfair & Co., Gun and Fishing Tackle Makers below, continuing this firm's westward march. Playfair's premises at No 142 were acquired in 1925 by the old established firm of George Jamieson 'jeweller to the Queen', not that Jamieson was still around. William Whyte Carry had purchased his business at 125 Union Street in 1908, but it was not until 1933 – the bicentenary of the original founding of the firm – that the firm's name was changed to Jamieson & Carry. This marked the arrival of W W Carry's son, Joseph Robert, as a partner. The Carrys are one of those remarkable family firms, now in their fourth generation. David Carry, the swimmer – son of Peter, a British champion skier – continues the link with precious metals. He won two gold medals at the 2006 Commonwealth Games, and took part in the 2008 Beijing Olympics.

Trinity Hall

This takes us across to the south side and we go back in time now to 8 September 1848 to join Queen Victoria and Prince Albert as they drive up Union Street for the first time, en route for a Balmoral Castle they had yet to see. A dazzling edifice caught Albert's eye on the south-east corner of Union Bridge, opposite the Aberdeen Hotel. It was embellished with pinnacles, battlements, stained-glass windows with a hint of the medieval in their tracery, all underlining the ancient origins of the Seven Incorporated Trades whose new headquarters this was. 'Who is the architect of this fine building?' the Prince asked. And so a week later the city architect John Smith and his son and partner William, for it was they, were summoned to the old castle and commissioned to design a new, more spacious, more prestigious Balmoral Castle.

John died in 1852 but William Smith, who had had a major hand in the design of the Trades Hall, carried out the Balmoral commission in 1855.

The first headquarters of the Seven Incorporated Trades, old 'Tarnty Ha' had developed out of the ruins of the old Trinity Friars Monastery near the foot of the Shiprow. It was demolished in 1845 to allow for the laying out of Guild and Exchange Streets, but the Trades had already secured one of the finest sites in Union Street for their second Trades Hall, which was renamed Trinity Hall in memory of the old monastery in 1908. It was on the first floor and was spectacular. A central door, still there, gave access via a staircase to the Great Hall with its stained glass, chandeliers, portraits, and hammerbeam ceiling.

Trinity Hall and Union Bridge, around 1870. James Lumsden & Co., Tailors & Clothiers, had taken over from James Littlejohn as ground floor tenant at No 155. There is a matching extension to the rear, and Hadden's Wool Mill looms up from the Green. The perfect symmetry of the buildings east of Trinity Hall is evident. The chairbound statue of Prince Albert is at the extreme left.

The upper vestibule and entrance to Trinity Hall.
The mural, centre top, represents the shoemaker trade, one of six painted in the 1930s, probably by students of Grays School of Art.

The ground floor was let to two shops. No 151 was occupied by M Rettie & Sons, 'silversmiths, jewellers and dealers in London and Geneva watches, clocks and fancy goods', while Mr Littlejohn had taken his fancy worsted warehouse across to No 155. He had perhaps detected an address even more prestigious than the Aberdeen Hotel building. The south side of Union Street from its early days was regarded as the popular side for shops.

The foundations deep down in the Denburnside (Denburn Road) provided space for the tenants' workshops, vaults and storage. The Incorporated Trades School was also located in the depths and was entered from the Denburn Road through the Trades' original ornate gateway, painstakingly moved from old 'Tarnty Ha'. In the 1890s, Lumsden's was succeeded at No 155 by McMillan's popular department store, which twenty years later acquired No 151 as well. 'McMillan's of Union Bridge' sold jewellery, clocks, luggage, china, prams, umbrellas, sports goods and gifts of all sorts on the ground and lower floors. As inveterate advertisers, McMillan's managed to create the impression that they owned Trinity Hall, if not Union Bridge.

Union Bridge

We move on to Union Bridge itself now. In the early 1800s, Thomas Telford ordained that the width of the Bridge be forty feet, rather than the seventy feet that Thomas Fletcher had indicated in his plans. This produced a very narrow bridge indeed, but Telford was adamant that the bridge must make a statement. It must look like a bridge.

In 1868, with the increase in population and traffic, Dean of Guild Jamieson argued that the bridge should be widened – 'at its widest it is much too narrow'. He was merely repeating what had been said many times before. Subsequent proposals to widen the bridge in 1874 and 1888 came to naught. After much discussion and the appointment of Special Committees, further remits, Acts of Parliament and the advent of Sir Benjamin Baker of Forth Bridge renown as advising engineer, widening by means of steel arches was agreed. But public opinion, vociferous and sustained, made it clear that in Aberdeen nothing would do for the widening of the bridge but granite. So be it.

In August 1905 the Improvements Committee were able to report that eleven tenders had been lodged and that the cost of the scheme would be in the region of £20,000. The Council took fright, quickly opting instead for the steel arch rib system. They accepted the lowest tender, that of George Hall, Builder, at £6,518 2s 11d. By the end of 1907, Hall's men had done their work. The great steel arches, and the horizontal girders that were to carry the new footway, had been manoeuvred into place. The original integrity and elegance of the bridge was lost, thanks to this steel corset.

Union Bridge goes into its steel corset, in 1907.

The Bridge's saving grace, its new cast iron parapet and lamps, were designed by the architect, Dr William Kelly. The leopard finials of the parapet, usually associated with Kelly, were the work of Sidney Boyes of Gray's School of Art and cast by William Wilson of Hay and Lyall.

Kelly's famous involvement came later. During one Aberdeen University Charities Week, students tied ribbons round the leopards' neck, and the great man, furious at such irreverence, ordered the ribbons to be removed. Thereafter they became 'Kelly's Cats'.

Sidney Boyes designed bronze panels as central features for the bridge, one for each side. The north panel shows draped allegorical figures representing Education, centre, flanked by Experience, Inspiration, Music, Literature, Science, Painting and Sculpture. It seems to have been painted with tar, perhaps to deter scribblers. Two of Kelly's Cats are on guard.

Palace Hotel

We can cross now to the south-west end of the bridge. Bridge Street, laid out in 1867, provided not only a new link between town and railway, but also created two new corner sites with Union Street, in the very heart of the city. The corner nearest Union Bridge was acquired in 1873 for new premises by John Keith of the go-ahead firm of drapers and silk mercers, Pratt & Keith, which had outgrown its Union Street premises just west of the Adelphi. The architect was James Matthews and the builder was Adam Mitchell. Pratt & Keith's premises occupied the whole length of the building on the ground floor. Their extensive wholesale business was housed in three floors below ground and there were two millinery workshops on the first floor. Six smaller shops occupied the lower reaches of the Palace Buildings, and Lorimer's boot and shoe shop stood on the east side. Apart from the Union Street frontage, the building itself ran about half the way down Bridge Street.

It was James Matthews who suggested that, instead of giving the remaining floors to office and residential accommodation, he should create a first-class hotel there. And so the Palace Hotel came into being, a fine essay in Scots baronial, turreted, with dormers terminating in thistle finials. If Trinity Hall, on the east side of Union Bridge, was the mother of Balmoral Castle, the Palace Hotel on the west was one of the daughters.

The original Palace Hotel, with Pratt & Keith on the ground floor. Lorimer's boot and shoe shop was on the east side. A M Mackie was the lessee.

The aftermath of the Palace Hotel fire, 1941. *The Palace had been a railway hotel for some years, with an extra storey added. The view to the right is down Bridge Street.*

In 1891, the Palace Buildings were acquired by the ever-ambitious Great North of Scotland Railway (GNSR) which embarked on an energetic programme of refurbishment, adding a further additional floor, altering the appearance of the Palace from a Scots baronial pile to a handsome and lofty Victorian railway hotel. Everything was of the finest: walls of marble, floors of marble mosaic, a frieze by James Bannochie & Sons, whose skilled plasterwork was a feature of many of the new West End residences, sumptuous silk Japanese wallpaper, urinals of marble and porcelain. The hotel became one of Aberdeen's most famous landmarks, the *de rigueur* stopover for royalty, the rich and the famous, everyone from Tyrone Power to Ramsay MacDonald.

One macabre episode lingered long in the memory of older Aberdonians. In the early years of the century, they turned out in numbers to look at peat, some said lead, spread outside the hotel over Union Bridge to deaden the sound of traffic. A millionaire American guest was gravely ill inside. 'But he died just the same, for a' his money,' as folk said.

On the night of 30/31 October 1941, the Palace Hotel burnt down, and six women members of staff, sleeping in the attics, lost their lives. In spite of a smell of burning, hotel staff were slow to react. The blackened ruins, sometimes mistaken for bomb damage, dominated Union Street during the war years. In 1945 the owners, the LNER, successors to the GNSR, announced plans to rebuild the hotel which, even before the fire, had become somewhat rundown. The plans never went ahead and in 1950 the building was completely demolished. Seven years later, the Dutch-owned C & A Modes built and opened their store on the site. While the drapers and railway managers who had built the Palace Hotel favoured a self-confident splendour, the directors of C & A opted for a building of plain mediocrity. Town planners of the day would not permit the firm's rainbow logo to be displayed. It was considered too garish for Union Street. How times have changed.

The 'Shargar Shoppies'
While the C & A scheme was underway, sharp-eyed developers spotted a promising 'gap site', the air space above the Bridge over the railway between Trinity Hall and C & A Modes. Permission was granted for the erection of seven shops in the gap, and by 1961 work was underway. The bridge's southern bronze panel, showing Commerce and her cohorts, was removed, along with all Kelly's Cats on this side of the bridge. They were re-erected in the Duthie Park, which has become a sort of Garden of Remembrance for such relics, dislodged from their original place by the course of progress.

In September 1963, an epic undertaking began which sent the city centre into a state of chaos. Two massive steel girders, which would support the new shops, were lowered into place. The shops of the Portacabin school of architecture, unkindly if accurately described by Alexander Scott in his great poem, 'Heart of Stone' as 'shargar shoppies' were duly airlifted into place.

Bonnieness-blind, thae folk for aa thir birr!
Wha else, i the stanie straucht o Union Street,
Wi only ae brig till open space
Wad block thon brichtness out wi shargar shoppies?

birr: energy
shargar: paltry, feeble

It was not the people of Aberdeen who blocked out the south side of the bridge, but in the words of Alexander Keith: 'Big Business as licensed by the Town Council'.

The bronze panel which was moved from the south side of Union Bridge to the Duthie Park in the early 1960s. It shows the allegorical figure of Commerce, centre, with Horn of Plenty, flanked by Agriculture, left, and the Sea right. Shipbuilding and Engineering are among the other figures depicted.

Crowds enjoying a pipe band display in Union Terrace Gardens in 1964. In the background, centre, shops are in the course of construction on Union Bridge. C&A Modes, which replaced the Palace Hotel, looms up on the right. Below it, on the other side of Union Street is the last remnant of the Doocot Brae.

The eastern end of Union Bridge, 1937. This photograph shows a fine, original seven-window block just east of McMillan's. Birrell the confectioner was at No 145 and Goodsons dress shop at No 149, with an original arcade-style doorway between them, leading to a Temperance Hotel above. McMillan's begins to appear at the right. The stained glass windows of Trinity Hall, above, are still intact.

On the south side of the bridge Saxone, R S McColl, Willoughby Tailoring, Chelsea Girl and Pizza Hut all became tenants in the early days. Other developers had been alerted to the possibility of spoils and the north side of the bridge came under attack in 1963 and again in 1966. Schemes were mooted for hotels, shops and car parks which would nicely blot out the fine and famous view of Union Terrace Gardens, His Majesty's Theatre and the Backs of Belmont. There had been much opposition to the south side scheme, yet it had gone ahead. The north side scheme was greeted with greater hostility still, and even philistines on the Council decided that enough was enough.

Back at the McMillan's end of Union Bridge, there had also been controversial developments. The Birrell–Goodsons building on McMillan's east side had become run down and was earmarked for demolition after the war. It was announced that a branch of the Littlewoods chain store would move into custom-built premises on the site, causing consternation among Aberdeen shoppers. The quality of the new building was not so much considered in those days as the query: was Littlewoods good enough for Union Street? Whatever the reservations about the siting of the store, the structure which replaced the original buildings after 1965 was architecturally disappointing.

Parking problems and rising rates had prompted the Incorporated Trades to move to a new Trinity Hall on the Great Western Road/Holburn Street corner. They had sold their Union Street property to Littlewoods, who planned to extend, and the Secretary of State had granted permission for the entire Trinity Hall building to be demolished. It is to the credit of the Moores family and the Littlewoods organisation that they listened to local conservationists. They worked out a scheme with city architects whereby Trinity Hall itself would be retained and restored, while the site could simultaneously be developed as an extension to the existing Littlewoods store. The Hall's original chandeliers and a facsimile of the original frieze were painstakingly recreated, a new co-ordinating carpet was woven, and Trinity Hall re-emerged in all its new splendour in November 1980, as the Trinity Grill restaurant. Apart from the frontage and the refurbished Trinity Hall/Grill, the rest of the building was demolished and a Littlewoods self-service restaurant was created next to the Trinity Grill. For a short time, the craft murals which could not be removed from the walls of the upper vestibule could be seen from the Denburn Road, high aloft, open to the winds, a lingering memorial. The McMillan's shop front at No 151 was removed as part of the extension programme, and the space became a window looking through to the main Littlewoods store.

Trinity Hall c1960, with McMillan's department store occupying the whole of the ground floor and still trading. The Goodsons-Birrell building, left, is about to be demolished. Saxone, extreme left, has survived for the moment.

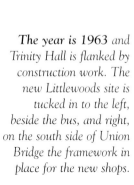

The year is 1963 and Trinity Hall is flanked by construction work. The new Littlewoods site is tucked in to the left, beside the bus, and right, on the south side of Union Bridge the framework in place for the new shops.

It is 1974, and this must be one of these 'Aberdeen on a flag day' pictures. Littlewoods is now in business. McMillan's is long gone, with No 151 boarded up. Timpson Shoes which latterly occupied No 155 is still trading. In the years that followed, the Trinity Hall building stood grimy and forlorn.

The south side of Union Bridge *with the original shops towards the end of their days. Littlewoods and Trinity Hall to the left.*

Further Developments

In 1974, a further development of the air space on the south side was mooted by Atholl Developments Ltd. The project was taken over by Norwich Union in 1982 and renamed the Trinity Shopping Centre. It opened in 1984, built with 'high tech' expertise over railway land above the Inverness line from the Wapping Street/Bridge Street intersection to Littlewoods. The sheer bulk of the development is best appreciated from Guild Street. Waterstone's and HMV opened on the Bridge, incorporated as part of the Centre, doing away with the 'shargar shoppies'.

The former Trinity Hall, above the former Timpson Shoes at No 155, right. This is now an entrance to the 'Shopping Centre,' i.e. the Trinity Centre (now Mall). Similarly, the former entrance to McMillan's at No 151, left, became a shop window for Littlewoods (out of sight), subsequently replaced by Primark.

The south side of Union Bridge today. *The bridge has been obliterated by a gimcrack display of clashing red, pink and magenta signs whose focal point is a big red, blue and yellow plastic T, right, the whole surmounted by sail-like awnings which seem to have jammed. At the Bridge Street end, C & A joined the exodus to the Bon Accord Centre and its former premises have become a Travelodge.*

The Trinity Centre and the Littlewoods extension were separate developments, but the firms involved collaborated. The space created by the demolition of Timpson Shoes at No 155 became an entrance to the Centre – now called 'The Mall, Aberdeen', which put an end to the ancient Trinity connection. Littlewoods closed in 2006 and the store became a branch of Primark. Trinity Hall remains part of these premises but is not open to the public. It is currently 'decommissioned' and there are no immediate plans for its use.

The North-West Corner

Finally, to the north-west corner, the highest point above the Denburn ravine, once the
Doocot Brae. In September 1745, during the Jacobite Rising, the brae briefly became a
cantonment for Major John Cope's 2,000 Hanoverian troops, who infamously trampled down
the crop ripening there, dismantled the city's cannon, confiscated all arms, and left the town
defenceless.

Harry Lumsden of Belhelvie Lodge, advocate and county bigshot, built a turreted
townhouse, No 1 Union Terrace, at what was the top of the old Doocot Brae, before the
terrace was finished. It is shown on page 76, top left. Here the family overwintered, made
social visits and held balls, and here Lumsden and his sons saw their clients and carried on
their business. In 1854, the family leased No 1 to the Northern Club, and nine years later,
from an upper window and on a day of endless civic speeches, prayers and unceasing rain,

Queen Victoria unveiled a bronze statue of her beloved Albert by Baron Carlo Marochetti. Though tall and manly in life, Prince Albert was sculpted in sedentary mode, overwhelmed by his massive chair, giant plaid, high boots, chains of office, scroll and hat of drooping feathers. Her Majesty did not seem too pleased with the ensemble, which is shown on page 80. In 1914, to make way for his son King Edward VII, Albert was carted off to the Union Terrace Gardens spur, where he remains. By 1874 the Northern Club, now Royal, had flitted west to Crimonmogate's House, just west of the Music Hall.

Considerable controversy surrounded the choice of this site for Edward VII, but Colonel Thomas Innes of Learney, senior Royal Archer during the king's last visit to Scotland, was in charge of the project, the Scottish Memorial to His Majesty. Innes was determined on the Union Terrace corner and was not a man to be gainsaid.

The former Doocot Brae. This photograph offers a sweeping view over the railway – the north line, which has tamed the Denburn Ravine – Union Terrace and the Gardens, which sit at the original medieval level of the town and are unique. Edward VII has replaced Prince Albert. Schemes for building over Union Terrace Gardens persistently materialise, and are inevitably opposed.

UNION STREET, ABERDEEN, LOOKING W., FROM UNION BRIDGE. 3936. G.W.W.

A general view looking west, 1890s. *Union Bridge has not yet been widened, though that causes no problems. The Palace Hotel has gone up a storey and opposite, Albert still skulks in his chair, below the magnificent Monkey House. Almost opposite the tram, right, is Mrs Bremner of Learney's grand portico.*

CHAPTER FIVE

ARCHETYPAL ABERDEEN

'The men hurry and have importance in their looks: and the young ladies march through Union Street in files like well-booted grenadiers.'

Professor Blackie, 'Two Great Northern Universities', Tait's Edinburgh Magazine, May 1833

The South Side: From Bridge Street to Crown Street

The photograph opposite was taken in the late 1890s, when the trams had not yet been electrified, but were drawn by horses. On the south side, beyond the Palace Hotel at the extreme left, a fine building, Nos 167–9 Union Street, keeks out at the top of the newly laid-out Bridge Street.

Wyllie's, bookseller to Her Majesty, is in residence, having arrived in 1870, when the building was new. Wyllie's had moved westwards, keeping step with Union Street, first to No 43 in 1814, then to No 51 in 1834, on to No 111 in 1847 and now in 1867 to what would later become Pegler's greengrocer and fruiterer at the corner of Bridge Street and Union Street. David Wyllie, the founder, had died in 1844, and his son James, a chip off the old block, was in charge. His rivals, A & R Milne, booksellers, were as usual a stone's throw away, at the far end of the row. Apart from the Wyllie's building and Canada House at the Crown Street end, this was a terrace of six original buildings, built post-1824, mostly with two shops on the ground floor and offices above. An exception was the Picture House, not in existence when this photo was taken.

By 1908, Wyllie's had been succeeded by the equally nomadic westbound Pegler's. George Pegler had opened his first fruit shop at 38 Broad Street in 1841, and there were other shops, later, further west in Union Street. But this popular shop on the Bridge Street corner, dark and earthy, is always remembered as *the* Pegler's, though it was also associated with the Thomson family for many years. The queue for bananas here was a regular feature of life in Aberdeen after the 1939–45 war and on one occasion there was a great hoo-haa when a woman was seen in the street outside eating a banana, which were then only available on children's green ration books.

Pegler's stayed until the 1960s and was succeeded by the dress chain, Etams, who initially favoured a quite stylish black décor, but in more recent times it and its successors, both

The queue at Pegler's, 1946. *People queued for bananas when they were still rationed. The door, which used to be at the angle of the building, has been moved round into Union Street. It is now back at the angle.*

outdoor clothing chains, have opted for the very deep fascias that are now common. The upper floors are entered from Bridge Street and have had a number of tenants over the years, at time of writing, an Italian restaurant. A seat by the window provides a safe view of the Union Street action of a Saturday evening.

Pegler's most enduring neighbour was Kennaway at No 173, one of Aberdeen's quartet of private bakers, along with Mitchell & Muil, Strathdee, and Ledingham. Kennaway had a handsome frontage, a pink granite fascia with leaded glass in the window. The baker's Luncheon, Smoking and Tea Rooms were advertised as 'the finest suite of Rooms in the City'. The shop itself was spacious and the restaurant lay behind it. For many years, a series of shoe shops occupied the premises next door at No 175. John Dunn, making his way west, was followed by Manfield, then Dolcis. Marshall & Philp, ironmongers, had been at No 179 as long as anyone could remember, i.e. before the First World War. Before that, they had been near the Stairs leading to the Green. Abbey (formerly National), Past Times and Game Station are to be found in this stretch now.

Nos 167–9 Union Street and Nos 2–4 Bridge Street. *Pegler's occupied much of the ground floor at Nos 167–9 Union Street and Nos 2-4 Bridge Street. The scale of this new building was right for the prominent corner where Union Street and Bridge Street meet. The angle is emphasised by pairs of windows at the first and second floors, complete with little balconies, while the top storey boasts three windows below a curving gable, flanked by two slender chimneys. The effect is pleasing, were it not for oversize, shiny fascias, and the general aura of dinginess, disappointing in such a prominent building. We have a good view of how well this building turns the corner down into Bridge Street.*

Beyond Marshall & Philp was the town house of the Misses Turner of Turnerhall. It had been No 173, but after renumbering became No 181. By 1902, the Turner ladies had gone and James Macbeth, the pianoforte-maker, was *in situ*. He was a prolific advertiser. Everyone knew Macbeth. My elderly aunt told me that as a girl she was convinced that he was also the Macbeth in the Shakespeare play. There could not be two Macbeths. He initially shared the premises with E Wadsworth & Bros, well known organ-builders, and the old townhouse would have afforded ample room in its lower floors for workshops. The piano, of course, was the equivalent of TV, the CD, the DVD and Aberdeen had a fair number of piano-makers and sheet-music-sellers and none more prominent than Macbeth's neighbours, Marr, Wood & Co. Their advertisements announced that they had been established in 1826. But which one? John Marr, who started off as a piano-tuner, had his pianoforte saloon at No 218 Union Street from the 1840s, perhaps earlier. Meanwhile, Wood & Co.'s saloon was at Nos 211–3, later the Grill public house from the 1850s. By 1890 there was amalgamation; Marr and Wood were together at No 183, next to Macbeth and his pianofortes at No 181. It looked like a cosy relationship.

In 1913, however, there was a great upheaval. Macbeth and his pianofortes moved, almost as far west as Collie's, (later Waterstone's). No 181 had been acquired for Ralph Judd's Associated Provincial Picture House. After visiting badly ventilated halls in England, Dr Judd vowed to put a good cinema in every major town. And so the Picture House arrived.

Like Macbeth the pianoforte-maker, the Picture House knew how to publicise itself. A banner would be suspended from the top storey of the building – from the manager's flat, in fact – to promote the current attraction. One is visible on the front cover of this book. The banner for the 1927 silent movie, *Ben Hur*, starring Ramon Navarro, used to be recalled by older folk, and in 1931, a large and grotesque model of a wingless plane in the foyer drew attention to a forthcoming blockbuster, Howard Hughes' *Hell's Angels*. There were also live shows. In 1926 Madame Isobel Murray, local teacher of ballroom dancing, demonstrated the Charleston.

Queuing at the Gaumont, formerly the Picture House, in 1957. Also visible from left, Kennaway, the baker and confectioner, Manfield & Sons shoe shop and Marshall & Philp, ironmongers.

Though custom-built as a cinema, the Picture House never quite shook off its domestic aura. The foyer, where a fire was lit on cold evenings, had been the front room of No 181. I can still remember the empty grate, though the fire was before my time. Then it was downstairs to the auditorium, built on the sloping ground between Union Street and Windmill Brae, where small cottages had to be demolished to accommodate the auditorium. A thick velvet curtain was taken aside by the usherette to give access to the stalls where all seats were one shilling and ninepence. The Picture House was not cheap. Tall pillars ran up to the balcony as they do in some churches, though here there were non-ecclesiastical seats for two. Another thick velvet curtain was discreetly drawn over the door of the Ladies' just outside the auditorium.

By 1950 the Rank Organisation had taken over and the name changed to Gaumont. Unaware of the manoeuvrings of the film industry, I much preferred the old one. More interesting was the conversion of a defunct tearoom on the first floor into a small art gallery. It was a dark, rather makeshift place, but very popular with local artists, Somewhere in Aberdeen, at last, where they could show their work! Among exhibitors in the first year, 1951, were Joan Eardley and the ABBO group, Eric Auld, Bill Baxter, Donny Buyers, and Bill Ord.

Marr Wood & Co, still at No 183, had amalgamated in 1925 with Paterson & Sons, also well known in the Aberdeen music business. At school all requirements for the singing class had to be purchased from Paterson, Sons & Marr Wood Ltd, 'piano-makers to H. M. the King', one of whose advertisements featured a grand piano in a spacious showroom with fluted Corinthian columns. Caroline Gimingham of Aberdeen Civic Society has written:

> You could spend many a happy afternoon listening to gramophone records before actually buying them. Upstairs was a series of rooms for piano practice for those who had no piano at home; and there was always the sound of tinkling pianos, with *Jesu, Joy of Man's Desiring* mingling with relentless scales-practice.

By the 1950s, the firm had replaced its dignified frontage for one perhaps inspired by R S McColls, newsagents, who had arrived next door. Paterson Marr Wood had gone by the 1960s. I have a feeling they had white goods in the window before the end. Dixons moved in, here or next door.

The Gaumont closed in 1973. Planning permission for a new block of shops and offices on the site was granted. No 181 was subsequently rebuilt and at time of writing houses Rosebys, with its pavement-level display of bedding, and Coral, the bookies. Currently Ann Summers, with its relentless display of immodest underwear, is on the old Paterson Marr Wood site and a hairdresser with the now normal giant fascia has replaced R S McColls. At No 187, the Edinburgh Woollen Mill shop (full marks for an attractive fascia) has replaced Morrisons.

The year is 1969 and this is surely one of these Aberdeen on a house-to-house collection day photos! Across the road, the Gaumont has eschewed its promotional banner and sports a two-storey- high neon sign. Peter Mitchell, tobacconist, is the small shop next door, then Paterson, Sons & Marr Wood, music-sellers, an R S McColl, and just before the arcaded door, Morrison's Gowns, a fashion shop which arrived about 1950. It belonged to the Paige group and was one of my favourites. It had an arcade displaying the pick of the newly arrived fashions. Annoyingly hidden by the No 24 Braeside bus are A & J Smith, jewellers, and Gordon & Smith, grocers.

Towards the end of the row came two shops both of which went back a long way. A & J Smith, jewellers, had arrived at No 191 by 1890. The firm, whose first shop was in St Nicholas Street, specialised in timeless Celtic pieces, river pearls and Cairngorms, as well as conventional gold watches and diamond rings. Being sent to collect a repair was always a special occasion. The atmosphere was calm and soporific, with only the sound of clocks peacefully ticking. While waiting for a tram, one could shelter in the doorway, cheered by a glimpse of A & J Smith's fire burning merrily in the grate.

Rosebys and Coral are on the Gaumont site now, breaking the skyline of the terrace with their mansard. This would not have been permitted by the New Street Trustees, even west of Union Bridge! To the right, Ann Summers, Super Cuts and the Edinburgh Woollen Mill.

Their neighbours at Nos 195–7 were Gordon & Smith, grocers, a long shop with a long history. The Gordons had been in the area since the 1840s. Thomas Snr, a merchant, had laid out Gordon Street on the other side of Langstane Place, for weaving sheds which would pay him a nice rent. Gordon & Smith, grocers, date from 1857 and by the early twentieth century were at Nos 195–7. In relatively modern times this building had a distinctive art deco frontage with arches, and inside, on a high ledge, blue and white eighteenth-century Chinese porcelain vases. They were popular, high-class grocers. At the left-hand counter numerous male assistants were in attendance, all clad in grey overall jackets and grey aprons, patient and ready to write out the orders of their clientele. Important housewives would sit down to dictate their needs, smoking a cigarette all the while. The right-hand counter, staffed by female assistants, was for cake, biscuits and confectionery. By the mid-1960s, Gordon & Smith had moved to the west end of Union Street, near Holburn Junction. Things were never quite the same again.

Laura Ashley was hereabouts before moving off to the Bon Accord Centre and in 1998 John Smith & Son, the Glasgow booksellers, opened a shop at No 195, reinforcing their upper floor and that of their neighbour, Kaye Shoes, which they had taken over, to support the weight of books and bookshelves. Bookshop and shoe shop collaborated to produce co-ordinated frontages, with arcade-style doors and matching fascias, showing what could be done with a little bit of imagination. Alas, John Smith eventually went out of business and other retailers moved in, though the rhythm of the two shops keeping time together has not altogether been lost.

The twin shops at No 195–7. *Although the twinned look devised by John Smith & Son booksellers, has been lost, Clarks and First Choice still give some indication of how good it could look. Canada House, at the right, is now occupied by the Bank of Scotland. First Choice has now gone.*

A fine building, Canada House, sits at Nos 199–203 on the Crown Street corner, which it turns gracefully. It was commissioned by the Scottish Canadian Mortgage Coy in 1893 and designed by the architects Ellis & Wilson whose offices were once nearby at No 181a. It has the look of a rather grand house with central first floor bay windows on both the Union Street and Crown Street elevations. On the top floor the dormers are hidden by a stout balustrade decorated with urns, large and small. The ground floor has a double frontage, Nos 199 and 203, while the central door at No 201 led to offices, on the upper floors. No 199 was occupied by a hatter and hosier, a wine merchant, a tailor, and from 1936 until 1968, the well-remembered gents' outfitters, Reith Brothers. The west end branch of the Union Bank of Scotland was at No 203, on the Crown Street corner, from the 1870s, dating back to the days of the original building, and remained a tenant at that number after Canada House was built.

By 1935, however, the Union Bank had crossed Dee Street to No 207 in the next block, which in accordance with bank practice, was dubbed the Union Bank Buildings. John Smith, Wools, Ltd, stockists of knitting wool and more specialist materials like tapestry thread became tenant at No 203 henceforth a Mecca for North East needlewomen. Smith's had a spinning wheel as their shop sign, and I always looked out for it when my bus, the 6A to Duthie Park turned into Crown Street. They took it with them when they moved to Bridge Street in 1948, and the British Linen Bank then occupied No 203. In a move of a different sort, the Bank of Scotland merged with the Union Bank in 1952 and replaced it at No 207, now renamed Bank of Scotland buildings. In 1971, back at Canada House, the Bank of Scotland took over the British Linen Bank, and with Reith gone and the Linen Bank swallowed up, the Bank of Scotland eventually left No 207 to occupy the double frontage of Canada House. Thus ends the bank musical chairs for the moment. Plans to turn Canada House into a pub in the 1999s have not been much heard of recently. Finally, a surprise may await those travelling up Crown Street as they pass the back of Canada House near the top of Windmill Brae, provided it is dark, and someone is working late at the rear of the Bank of Scotland with the lights on. There may well be a sudden and joyful vision of stained glass windows.

The North Side
From Union Terrace to South Silver Street
Harry Lumsden of Belhelvie's townhouse stood at No 1 Union Terrace for some eighty years, then the site was subsequently acquired for the Northern Assurance Company, for their new headquarters. The building, designed by A Marshall Mackenzie, architect, John Morgan

CANADA HOUSE
201

The Bank of Scotland's Red Indian at Canada House, carved in contrasting pink granite.

master mason, reflected the confidence and aspirations of the city and its business community at this time. Built in 1885 of finely-axed Kemnay granite it is a superlative showpiece for the granite trade. The entrance is dominated by enriched Doric columns (egg and dart on the underside) and wrought iron gates, the latter a later addition, to keep the monkeys either in or out. The Monkey House, origin unknown, was the building's nickname. At street level the long windows are capped by triangular pediments on the Union Street side – and an ornate side entrance, leading upstairs, usually not noticed, has a semi-elliptical one. An inner door, of tatty plywood, usually on view, spoils the effect. The channelled stonework at ground floor level is quite spectacular. The myriad of detail on the Monkey House façade, the garlands decorating the frieze above the Ionic columns for example are best viewed from across Union Street.

The Monkey House

The Northern Assurance Company merged with the Commercial Union in 1968. Others mergers and takeovers followed, and No 1 Union Terrace ended its days as an insurance office after over hundred years on the site. In December 2003 the building re-opened as the Monkey House – the nickname is now official – which will not insure you, but will serve you a meal and a drink. The interior merits the highest Aberdeen accolade, 'nae bad', with its crowned columns of polished granite, ceiling of coffered panels, sumptuous friezes, walls lined with Canadian redwood and American white walnut. 'Heymin, faraboots is the lavvy?' a plaintive voice is heard calling. One cannot help but notice that Victorian banks and insurance company offices that are converted into pubs retain their magnificent interiors, while those that retain their original function are required to have interiors more suited to supermarket checkouts or betting offices, such are the demands of modern commerce.

Returning to the photo at the beginning of this chapter, the buildings between the Monkey House, right and the Music Hall, which went up during the 1820s-30s are still in their original state. Nothing as yet has shot upwards and we have a perfect terrace. No 148, the Cheltenham & Gloucester office, next door to the Monkey House is a neat original sliver. Here in the 1920s and thirties the Yorkshire Insurance Company, was on the ground floor, with restrained frontage, with Williamson Booth, Mintos and Morrison, solicitors and George Bennett Mitchell, architect above The buildings from No 150 up to North Silver Street are B-listed as a group. No 150 itself immediately east of Diamond Street started life as a tenemental double house, two short flights of steps over two basements, leading to two front doors with windows on either side, enclosed by its own railings, which survived longer than most.

The Monkey House, *one of Union Street's finest buildings with the Union Terrace façade to the right of the portico. It was originally built as the headquarters of the Northern Assurance Co. At the extreme right is the evil-looking Lloyds building. The 'neat original sliver' of the Cheltenham & Gloucester building is extreme left.*

No 150 *as a double house.* *It later became Café Ici and is now Society.*

No 150 used to operate as two sets of commercial premises with a diverse mix of tenants. For much of the second half of the nineteenth century, ladies' outfitters and milliners occupied the main premises, with a cab office at No 150½, probably the basement. The Perth Dye Works was at No 150 in the early twentieth century, and keeping the dyers company were William Brown & Co., fishing-tackle-makers, before they went to Belmont Street. The Deeside Dairy and a sewing machine agency were at 150b, with a window-cleaning company in the basement.

By the 1930s, Pat Grant, the well-known hairdresser, was working on two levels. The other occupants from then on were numerous insurance companies, including the Royal Exchange and the Liverpool, London & Globe which, with Pat Grant, endured until the mid-1950s, when there was a great makeover. The architect A G R Mackenzie, then quite elderly, created a new ground floor and elegant frontage, sweeping away the tenemental traces, the railings, the steps and exposed basements.

The elegantly transformed No 150 on the Diamond Street corner, with the Cheltenham & Gloucester office at the extreme right.

Immediately west of the junction with Diamond Street came a batch of townhouses. In the 1840s and 1850s, Mrs Bremner of Learney resided in the house near the corner, No 152, which boasted a splendid pillared portico, topped by a balustraded balcony. It can be seen in the first photo of this chapter, between the Monkey House and the Music Hall. But by the early 1860s, No 152, now grandly named the Royal Bank Buildings, had gone commercial and was occupied by the Royal Bank of Scotland. The bankers shared Mrs Bremner's pillared portico with the other tenants, Cochran & Macpherson, advocates, until it was removed. In 1956, after nearly ninety years at No 152, there came a swap. The Royal Bank and the lawyers crossed Diamond Street and took up residence at the architecturally enhanced No 150, which duly became the Royal Bank Buildings, while No 152 provided accommodation for insurance companies and other businesses. In recent years, No 150 became Café Ici, and is now Society, while No 152 is a branch of the fast food chain, Kentucky Fried Chicken.

The Hon. David Ogilvie of Clova had his townhouse at No 154 in the 1850s and 1860s, while Miss Ogilvie of Auchries was at No 156, succeeded by W J Lumsden of Balmedie. By the 1870s, David Fiddes, M D, one of a bourrachie of medics, was at No 154. Next door at No 156 were Francis Ogston, M D, first Professor of Jurisprudence at Aberdeen University, and his son, Dr Frank Ogston, later a lecturer in Medical Jurisprudence at Otago University, New Zealand. They were the son and grandson respectively of the famous 'Soapy' Ogston. Alexander Kilgour, M D, was at No 158.

Though all were still original houses, by the 1890s this row was taking on an increasingly commercial aspect, with Peter Clark's Shetland Warehouse and the Sixpenny Continental Bazaar replacing the Ogstons at No 156, stranding Dr Fiddes's daughter at No 154 between the Bazaar and the Royal Bank Buildings.

No 154 left after rebuilding in the early twentieth century. The Lakeland household shop is on the ground floor at the present time. Kentucky Fried Chicken is right on the Diamond Street corner at No 152.

In the early twentieth century there was some imaginative rebuilding. After Miss Fiddes left, her home was transformed into the amazing edifice we see today shown on page 113. On the first and second floors there are two stolid storeys of bay windows, topped by balustrades, while on the third and fourth, two fantastical storeys have flown in, straight out of *The Thousand and One Nights*. No exotic harems inside though, but there was once a cosy warren of student bedsits. On the ground floor, the handsomely appointed West End Café appeared at pavement level – 'nothing quite like it in Aberdeen', according to its advertisements.

The original West End Café entrance in the early twentieth century. Lakeland has carried out a neat reinstatement of its frontage, omitting the heavy pediment, as shown on page 113.

The West End Café was for many years a newspaperman's howff. It later became a branch of Mitchell & Muil's, bakers and takeaway. The entire building underwent interior reconstruction and one envisaged the emergence of a few spacious, luxury apartments with excellent views of Union Street. Disappointingly, the small flatlets which eventually materialised are approached via a back lane and tatty rear entrance. One bonus, however, has been remodelling at pavement level to provide a double frontage for the household shop Lakeland, including an excellent, restrained version of the old West End Café entrance.

Next door but one, No 158, an original, like No 154, also underwent a complete transformation. An asymmetrical pile emerged, restrained but quite chic, with a slim, campanile-like staircase tower on the east side. This features a delightful oriel window, complete with mini-battlement, on the first floor and is topped by an onion-style dome. On the ground floor was Strathdee's Restaurant – renamed the Palace Restaurant in the 1950s – a popular meeting place with function rooms upstairs. 'Open till 11pm, our Five Floors are at your service,' said the adverts.

Survivors of the original 1824–33 terrace blend with their high and mighty neighbours. No 158, centre, used to be the Palace Restaurant.

No 158 Union Street, formerly the Palace Restaurant. *It was once a popular rendezvous on the ground floor while the function rooms above hosted everything from birthday parties to Golden Wedding Anniversaries.*

Watt & Milne, 1955.

Today Caffè Nero has the ground-floor slot. Between the two lofty buildings, the Scottish Hydro-Electric Shop sits doucely at No 156, altered, of course, but still discernible as an original. The Corporation Electricity Department set up shop there in the 1920s.

Finally, on the corner with North Silver Street, are Nos 164–172, a six-window building dating from the 1830s, originally two houses. Over the years a variety of shops occupied the ground floor: a druggist, a watchmaker, even James Macbeth, the nomadic pianoforte-maker. James Henderson, photo dealers, were at No 164 from 1904, Pullars Dyeworks were at No 168 in the 1920s and Harrow the Florists from the 1930s. It is now a bookies with a fascia you can't fail to notice.

The upstairs floors were tenanted by the usual mix of the professional, the commercial and the residential. In the 1890s, a distinguished firm of architects, W & J Smith & Kelly, had offices at No 170. William and John Smith were the son and grandson of the great John Smith. Dr William Kelly, no less, had once been their apprentice and was now a partner.

Best remembered of the shops was Watt & Milne, silk mercers. They opened here in the 1880s, and at their zenith occupied Nos 166–172. The firm was older than Watt & Grant, almost as old as John Falconer. It was never the most fashionable of shops, on the 'wrong' side of Union Street as far as women shoppers were concerned and it was certainly not a young person's shop. I can only remember going in only once, in search of something elusive. I remember that the higher one climbed the more it resembled an attic dwelling rather than a shop. It was acquired by the House of Fraser in 1955, and an attempt was made to give it a lease of life as a babywear shop. It was sold by Frasers in 1967. A number of businesses have come and gone, but since 1998 Aberdeen Journals have run an attractive and successful retail department here, with local books, souvenirs, a travel agency, and, most important, the local daily papers and their back numbers.

Nos 207–219, *a neat little terrace with The Grill, centre.*

CHAPTER SIX

UNION STREET WEST

'The medical men who aimed at a West End practice dwelled in Union Street west of the bridge, for the current idea about that was that a West End practice would surely suffer if the professional plate were not exhibited in Union Street.'

Lachlan Mackinnon, Recollections of an Old Lawyer, 1935

The South Side: From Crown Street to Bon Accord Street

We move now into the western plain, leaving the Denburn ravine and its engineering problems behind. From the 1860s, for a relatively short period, the area between Crown Street and South Silver Street to Bon Accord Terrace and Summer Street, favoured by the genteel, was known as Union Street West.

This little terrace, opposite, Nos 207–219 Union Street, dating from the early 1830s, conformed neatly to the rules and regulations of the Union Street Trustees. If ever a restoration of Union Street were attempted, it could start here. Uniform dormers, blending colour schemes and fascias would work wonders. Today, at the Crown Street end, one starts with something unexpected – an escalator. A survivor from the old banking days, it takes one up to the bookmaker's shop in style. There's also a branch of R S McColls, a couple of travel shops, a mobile phone shop as one would expect – and the Grill.

The first building on the Crown Street corner was the shop belonging to Charles Davidson, pharmacist. Davidson had graduated in arts at Marischal College in 1828 and planned to go on to study medicine. Unfortunately, the summer before the start of the new session, his father, a timber merchant, lost his entire stock. The wood was lying in a holding pool on the Dee, waiting to be floated down to the harbour and sold. It was smashed to smithereens in the Muckle Spate of August 1829. Davidson Snr was bankrupted and unable to afford university fees. He apprenticed Charles to a pharmacist – the next best thing and much less costly. The young man thrived, had started up on his own by 1834 and was in Union Street by the early 1850s. His shop was excellently placed to serve the gentry who came into town via the new Skene or Deeside turnpikes to visit the County Rooms opposite. Numerous doctors had their practices in the area and Charles Davidson was ready to dispense medicines for those doctors who didn't dispense their own.

Charles was joined in partnership in 1867 by John P Kay, who had begun his career further down Union Street at much the same time. The words Davidson & Kay ('Chemists to the King') must be engraved on the hearts of many Aberdonians of a certain age, so well known did the firm become. While remaining in Union Street, they also expanded into the West End, first to Holburn Junction and then to Alford Place, where their immaculate displays of pharmaceutical bottles, carboys, beakers, and nests of little wooden drawers were testament to pride in their profession.

The firm prospered and Davidson became proprietor of Foresterhill House. Later Aberdeen Royal Infirmary was, one might say, incorporated into his grounds. By 1933, Davidson & Kay had swapped the Crown Street corner for No 219 at the Dee Street end, taking their mortar and pestle sign with them. This made way for the Union Bank of Scotland and the musical chairs which followed at Canada House. Edwards 'Sir' Shop replaced Davidson & Kay at No 219 in the early 1980s, about the time the Davidson & Kay business closed.

Other enduring residents included James Brown, fish and game dealer, originally at No 215, where he succeeded George Glegg & Sons, confectioners to the gentry, in the 1880s. Brown prospered and by 1920 had moved to No 209, next to Davidson & Kay. The angler with his deerstalker and bag, in bronze silhouette on the door, was a favourite Union Street icon for years. James Brown was there until the 1960s when Elena Mae, the camera shop, took over at that address.

Wood & Co.'s pianoforte saloon, managed by F H Lakin, was based at No 213 for a time. In 1877, Richard Benson, restaurateur, moved from Union Place, and set up a Grill Restaurant at No 213, where he was succeeded by William Anderson. The Grill Billiard Saloon – whose name was inspired by the restaurant – was in operation for a time, upstairs at No 211. Other the tenants around that time included the English watercolourist Robert Meadows, two solicitors, an architect and an investment company.

Jas Duthie, genteel fruiterer, had moved into No 215 in the 1930s, and was succeeded there by Pegler's, on the road again, in the 1960s. Much earlier, in the 1860s, James Cassie the wandering portrait painter, could be found in the rooms above No 215. The Grill, meanwhile, found its true forte as a favourite men-only pub – though ladies are now welcome, of course. In 1926, the bar was classily and simply refitted inside and out by Jenkins & Marr, architects, and it has stood the test of time. Internally the ceiling plasterwork, the mahogany-panelled walls and particularly the long bar counter are features of the place. The subdued oxidised bronze frontage is quite unusual, with frosted glass, fruity festoons, drops and patera. A good range of beer and lagers are available on draught and there is an exceptional selection of spirits. In 2008 The Grill was named Bar of the Year by *Whisky Magazine* in its 'Icons of Whisky' awards, not only for its collection of the craitur, but for 'its commitment and passion to educate the consumer'.

Dee Street to Bon Accord Street

We can now cross to the terrace once flanked by two great Aberdeen icons, Watt & Grant, general drapers, furriers and outfitters at the Dee Street side, and Andrew Collie, family grocer, wine merchant, cook, confectioner and Registry for Servants at the Bon Accord Street end – to give them their full titles of fifty years ago. At the Watt & Grant end was James Fraser, wine and spirit dealer, dating from the 1830s and probably the first occupant of the building on the Dee Street corner, Nos 221–3. By the 1840s, he was also in charge of the receiving Post Office located here. His neighbour at No 223 for many years was William Coutts, painter.

Union Street in 1869. This print shows much of the area covered in this chapter. Left, the two future Watt & Grant buildings, and beyond, the original row of terracing, of which a small portion remains. The house with the pillared portico was the Northern Hotel, later Collie's, presently Waterstone's. The Free West Kirk (now Soul) looms above, the embellishment of its spire quite brilliant, with crockets, pinnacles, lucarnes and criss-cross banding. Now much eroded, sadly. Right, the Music Hall, followed by a townhouse, No 198, later the YMCA, and Crimonmogate's House, later the Royal Northern Club. The original house on the Huntly Street corner beyond Crimonmogate's was replaced by the Royal Insurance Buildings, now Starbucks. The high house below the spire of Gilcomston Free (now South), is now the Skipton Building Society premises.

In 1882, Alexander Watt & John Grant set up their first premises in Union Street at Nos 225–7, (style of James Souttar around 1870), and by 1900 had acquired the Coutts and Fraser premises next door at Nos 221–3 as well, including the receiving Post Office. Their address became Nos 221–5. From the start, they created a high-class drapery aimed at a refined West End clientele, with door-girls greeting customers as they stepped from their carriages. They stocked upmarket labels including the whole Burberry range, from gowns to fur-lined coats and the 'charming, weather-proof urbitor'. By 1907, when Watt & Grant celebrated their 25th anniversary across in the West End Café, they had a staff of around 200.

Watt & Grant around the beginning of the twentieth century. The roof of the 1830s building, left, Nos 221–3, is already heightened. Cover the roof and the glass frontage and the original building appears. The first W&G building, Nos 225–7, right, still retains arcading on the ground floor. When the boards reading 'Dress, Mantle & Millinery Saloon' were taken down, large holes were left in the façade. These have been cleverly incorporated in decorative carving.

Watt & Grant was a constant of Aberdeen life, a must for window-shopping. Girls from neighbouring offices would dash across at lunchtime to view the new spring or autumn collections. W&G had a good haberdashery department, good-quality school uniforms, fabulous swimwear, and above all, outfits that were 'one-offs'. Buyers could select with their clientele in mind, and were not under compulsion to purchase an entire range. Gina Davies put on dazzling shows of millinery. There was even a floorwalker. For many ladies, Friday morning coffee with the 'girls' at Watt & Grant was a ritual not to be missed. The restaurant was at the top of the building and one stepped out of the lift straight into an amazing crescendo of sound. W&G had become a limited company by 1927 with Alexander's son A M (Sandy) Watt continuing as managing director, though he still described himself in the old style, as 'warehouseman'. He died in 1963, the last of a short line, but by then Watt & Grant had already been taken over by House of Fraser, in 1954.

Watt & Grant's neighbours were two terraced shops dating from the 1830s. At No 229 were A & R Milne, booksellers and stationers, with a busy newspaper kiosk, while Charles Michie, chemist, was next door at No 231. (Today these shops are occupied by Greggs the baker and CC respectively). C A Michie, who had qualified in pharmacy before the First World War, earlier had a business at No 123 Crown Street. He moved to Union Street in 1933, in succession to J D Duncan, chemist, who also ran the Union Street Post Office here, taking over from No 221, hence the pillar box outside. Post Offices and pharmacies so often went together, though Duncan's postal duties ended when the Crown Street Scots baronial GPO opened round the corner in 1908. Michie's, always innovative, were specialists in photography. After C A Michie's death in 1963, his sons, John and Charles, took over the business, acquiring more pharmacies. In 1976, they bought Ingasetter, whose products included Dee Lavender Water, and in 1978 they opened Country Ways in Holburn Street.

C A Michie's original frontage, with mortar and pestle aloft and pillar box outside. The entrance to the former surgery of Dr James Rice, father of Principal Duncan Rice of Aberdeen University, is at the left. The pillar box remains.

The buildings now change in style and the numbering suddenly jumps from No 231 to No 245, though there is no break in the street. In his *Recollections of an Old Lawyer*, Lachlan Mackinnon explains what happened. His father, also a lawyer, moved to Union Street in 1858 and bought No 233, the next house in the row, as a family home. Robert Ness, coachbuilder, had already built a house next door, and a carriage bazaar, presumably round at the back on Langstane Place, where there were numerous stables. Mackinnon Snr bought these premises and used Ness's house as his firm's office. The first Tramway Office was based here and both Mackinnons served as secretaries of the Aberdeen District Tramways Company, which ran the old horse trams. Later, Mackinnon Snr demolished these buildings and around 1890 built the high and handsome Mackinnon's Buildings, designed by the architect A Marshall Mackenzie, who chanced to have his own offices nearby. Following on from No 231, Mackinnon's Buildings numbered Nos 245–55. The numbers of the demolished buildings were simply omitted.

True to form, James Wyllie arrived at Mackinnon's Buildings, No 247, as soon as they were up, (with A & R Milne, booksellers, moving to No 229). By 1904, W J Milne, the hatter and hosier, arrived next door to Wyllie at Nos 249–51, which had an extensive frontage. Henderson, watch specialist, jeweller and owner of the giant clock, was at No 253 from 1930. Thus Mackinnon's Buildings hosted one of the most famous rows of shop fronts in Aberdeen.

Wyllie's was a household name. Operating as a bookseller for well over a century, it also published local-interest books by authors such as W Douglas Simpson and was a supplier of maps, white papers, stationery and school books, the latter admittedly to a captive clientele. But by 1940 the Wyllie family's interest had waned. Passing by one day and noticing a 'For Sale' sign, George Westland, advertisement manager for the old *Bon Accord*, bought Wyllie's on a whim. He became an enthusiastic bookseller and his son Alan joined the firm in 1949.

Mackinnon's Buildings were becoming increasingly costly to maintain and in 1965 the eastern section, the Milne–Wyllie building, was sold to the House of Fraser by its owners, Wyllie's, W J Milne and Bower & Smith, the accountants upstairs at No 245. Though Lord Fraser had acquired A & R Milne's bookseller as well as Watt & Grant, he had to loup Michie's to purchase the Milne–Wyllie building and did not have a clean sweep as he progressed westwards. C A Michie steadfastly refused to sell, much to the annoyance of the mighty draper.

Wyllie's and A & R Milne, rivals in life, were now united after death, forming Watt & Grant's Bookshop at the Wyllie shop with Alan Westland as general manager. A & R Milne's

The area in the 1980s with (top), Charles Michie, centre, sandwiched between a sea of Watt & Grants. Left of Michie's, A&R Milne's former bookshop has become an extension of W&G's. Right, Mackinnon's Buildings break into the original terrace with Watt & Grant's Bookshop on the ground floor. It was originally Wyllie's Bookshop. Below, the former Wyllie's is left while right, Watt & Grant's Bookshop has extended into the double-fronted shop that had previously been W J Milne, gents' outfitters.

Mackinnon's Buildings today. *The buildings are delineated by the massive doors at either side. The left-hand crest on the attic pediment is the boar's head crest for Mackinnon and on the right-hand, L McK for Lachlan Mackinnon. In 2008, the pilasters give a sense of soaring upwards, emphasised by the elegant Cruise frontage. W J Milne, the stylish men's outfitters used to be located here. Hugo Boss, left, occupies the former Wyllie's bookshop. The Austin Reed section, in separate ownership, took charge of the mighty clock after the departure of David Henderson the jeweller from No 253.*

YES! MILNE'S THE PLACE
JUST OPPOSITE THE CLUB

TELEPHONE
ABERDEEN
23950

•

TELEGRAMS
'GALLOWSES'
ABERDEEN

Established
1904

Men's Outfitters
W. J. MILNE, LTD
ABERDEEN

redundant shop had become part of W&G. Watt & Grant closed in 1981, (the unthinkable had happened) but the bookshop continued, eventually moving into what had once been W J Milne, who had departed to Albyn Place. Regrettably, in March 1986, Watt & Grant's bookshop closed, ending nearly a century of bookselling on the site. Watt & Grant's itself had been converted into offices with a Burger King on the ground floor. No more window-shopping.

Two fine buildings lay west of the Mackinnon's block. Both had co-ordinating balustrading and blending dormers; they were not identical yet had been given a feeling of unity. The first, Nos 257–9, was also built by A Marshall Mackenzie, about the same time as Mackinnon's Buildings, around 1890. At a later date, No 257 became James Allan, shoes. This was always enjoyable to visit, for it had a gallery that ran round the shop, with its own assistants, so one was never dependent on the vagaries of downstairs staff. This is now G-Star Raw. With the entrance to the Victoria House offices to the west, it makes a nicely co-ordinated unit, just as it was designed to be. Hopefully the days of Quid's In and the like are over.

The other building, Nos 261–3, designed in 1900 by A H L Mackinnon, is modest and elegant. For many years it housed Milne & Munro, of the famous golden boot, at No 263. This has now been replaced by Jones, bootmakers. No 261 has become a beauty clinic of dazzling whiteness. It was home, in its early days, to Alexander Murray, 'bookseller, publisher, stationer, librarian, news and railway and steamer agent, Tel No 6'. Murray, father of Madame Murray of ballroom-dancing fame, had set up here even before the Mackinnon's Buildings, and must have been less than amused to find Wyllie's and A & R Milne, the two best known booksellers in the city, moving in a matter of yards away. He stuck it out until the First World War, then moved across the road.

The upstairs offices of these three buildings, apart from the usual lawyers, accountants and architects, attracted an artistic clientele, including John M Aiken and Douglas Strachan, both stained-glass specialists, G R Gowans, and, until his untimely death in 1905, the gifted Robert Brough. William Swainson of the Music Department at Aberdeen University also had rooms here. In modern times Habitat was hereabouts.

Opposite, left, the world weary gentleman in the top hat posing outside the Royal Northern Club across the road from his shop featured in the distinctive advertisements of W J Milne, gent's outfitters. Right, One of Union Street's favourite icons, the golden boot, a traditional craftsman's sign was originally sited above Milne & Munro's shoeshop at No 263 and continues on guard above their successors, Jones, bootmakers.

Left. A Northern Hotel advertisement. No address necessary! It was a double house, complete with railings and sunks below. The principal entrance has a pillared portico. Right, Andrew Collie occupies the corner portion of the former Northern Hotel. The golden boot can just be made out above the neighbouring fascia.

Towards the end of the row, the number-changing demon is afoot, possibly the result of the MacKinnon's Buildings upheaval. Lachlan Mackinnon, writing in the 1930s about the 1860s, describes how the 'reconstructed building … subsequently the Northern Hotel … is now owned by Andrew Collie & Co. Ltd.' This building may have been the townhouse of the Davidsons of Dess before the reconstruction. The Northern Hotel, No 245, not to be confused with the famous hotel later established at Kittybrewster, was run by Mr and Mrs Mackie, who subsequently became lessees of the GNSR's Palace Hotel, while No 245 became the Collegiate School, run by Camille de Clayes, who later went off to be a wine merchant in London. His wife, Alice, lived in Rubislaw Den South.

Andrew Collie, the grocer, had arrived in the area in the 1880s. By 1917–8 he was at No 265, the smaller, eastern part of the Northern Hotel double building, formerly No 245. Pratt & Keith, formerly of the Palace Buildings, now occupied Nos 269–71 on the Bon Accord

Street side. This corner was not without its dangers. A stone falling from the spire of the Free West (now Soul) cracked one of Pratt & Keith's windows. By the late 1920s, Pratt & Keith had gone and Collie's had moved into the corner building that is always associated with it.

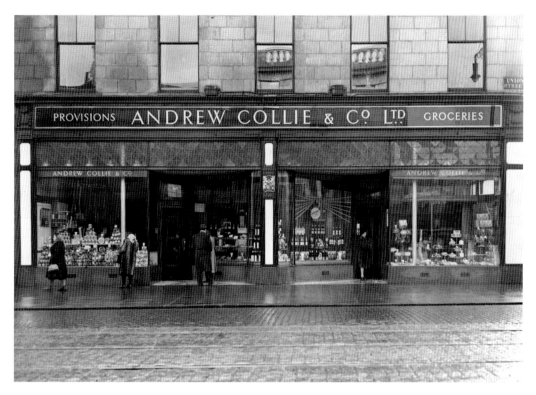

Andrew Collie & Co Ltd, 1950. *It had excellent, artistic window dressing with never a poster in sight. The balustrade of what is now the Skipton building is reflected in the gleaming upstairs windows.*

Collie's was always an early port of call during shopping expeditions. My mother would queue at the semi-circular counter by the window, where a superior member of staff – immaculate in chef's rig, minus hat – presided over the boiled ham and worked the great slicer. Cakes and biscuits were to the left of the ham counter, facing north, I think, with coffee and tea on the right. The shop was spacious and quiet, with models of sumptuous wedding cakes on display, and the air was famously permeated with the smell of roasting coffee beans. More activity went on behind the scenes for Collie's also supplied hotels and restaurants. One day I noticed a woman going into the Servants' Registry. Not aware of having seen a servant before, I stared and got a ticking off.

Collie's closed down in the early 1970s. The building later became Maples, a furniture shop, one of those places where the staff always seemed to be too busy to attend to customers. The double building was again 'reconstructed', perhaps with the aim of making it resemble a large modern office block with the aid of a modern attic storey, several courses of what looks like breeze block and a needless canopy, which became a victim of bashings from high-sided vehicles turning into Bon Accord Street.

The old Collie's as an office block. *Dillons bookshop was formerly on the ground floor, succeeded by Waterstone's.*

North Side: South Silver Street to Union Row

The Music Hall

We can now cross the road and go back in time to another procession on another day, 26 April 1820. It was wet and blustery and the fourth year of Aberdeen's bankruptcy. In defiance of the weather and the city's financial straits, a great procession of 1,500 freemasons had foregathered and processed along Union Street, taking up the entire road from the Castlegate to Union Bridge. Walking with them and carrying a set of plans was the architect, the thirty-year-old Archibald Simpson. 'Abidy was there', of course: the nobility, the county lairds, the city dignitaries, while 'an immense concourse' of people of all ranks crowded the streets, 10,000 all told, so it was said, while 'gay and elegant ladies' stood at windows and balconies. A halt was called where the newly laid-out Silver Street met Union Street. With the most elaborate of masonic ceremonies, the singing of the 'Masons' Anthem', the handing over of the square, the plumb, the level and the mallet to the appropriate dignitaries and a prayer to the Great Architect of the Universe, the foundation stone of the County or Assembly Rooms, later the Music Hall, was laid.

The 'Elevation and Ground Plan' for the County Rooms. The statues at the top of the building have not materialised.

This was one of the greatest processions Union Street had ever seen, yet the initiative that led to it was entirely due to the county lairds. 'After the building of Union Street,' the historian William Kennedy complained, 'unlike Edinburgh and Glasgow there were no public rooms for fashionable amusement.' Assemblies had to be held in taverns, 'which are ill-adapted for such a purpose'. Two attempts by the city to build assembly rooms failed for lack of funding, but in 1818, at the annual race meeting at the Links, the County launched a third attempt. By the end of that year, £7,000 had been subscribed and a committee headed by the Duke of Gordon was put in charge of the project. In an anonymous contest that attracted ten competitors, Archibald Simpson submitted the winning design, and by February he was taking in estimates for contracts.

The County or Assembly Rooms, built of Dancing Cairns granite at a cost of £11,500, were said to have made Simpson's reputation overnight. Beyond the massive portico, an elegant foyer awaited guests. A long promenade with a card room – a rotunda – and a supper room lay to the left (today these are the Round Room and Square Room). To the right was the ballroom (today toilets and cloakroom). At the end was the banqueting room, designed to seat up to 3,000. All rooms were linked by folding doors, the whole designed to allow the County to meet and mingle, which they did, holding brilliant suppers and balls at the time of the annual Race Meetings.

In 1858 the buildings, which had never cleared their debts, were sold to the newly-formed Aberdeen Music Hall Company. The architect, James Matthews, was commissioned to design the present Music Hall. The point of the exercise was to replace the banqueting room with a hall large enough to entice the great Victorian stars to Aberdeen, and to make their visits a financial success. It was not all musical entertainment, however. Prince Albert inaugurated both the Music Hall and the British Association's Annual Meeting in Aberdeen simultaneously in 1859. In 1899, the artist, Douglas Strachan, on the brink of success as a stained-glass artist, was commissioned to create a large mural scheme for the Music Hall. Five of his panels depicting the story of Orpheus survive.

By 1928, the Music Hall Company was in liquidation and the buildings and Willis organ were sold to Aberdeen Town Council for £34,000. In the years that followed, popular acts continued to come to the Music Hall. There were concerts by the Scottish National Orchestra and other leading ensembles; while the pianists Alfred Cortot and Moura Lympany and the folk singer Josh White of 'You Gets No Bread with One Meat Ball' fame were occasional visitors.

But there was a mixed bag of entertainments and no real focus. Dog shows jostled with boxing tournaments, sales of work with all-in-wrestling, Ideal Home Exhibitions with Trade Union Conferences. By 1960 the place had been allowed to deteriorate. It was cold and unwelcoming, the vestibule littered with milk crates and tacky chairs. It was attacked in the press as a white elephant. An Edinburgh development company picked up the scent of apathy and sought permission to demolish the Music Hall as part of a redevelopment scheme it proposed for Union Street.

It was not too late. A public controversy ensued and distinguished musicians waded in. The developers backed off. A second attempt was made in 1972, this time from the enemy within, to turn the Category A-listed building into a conference centre, necessitating the removal of the portico and the gutting of much of the interior, including the destruction of

Simpson's handsome rooms. A Public Enquiry quashed this display of philistinism from the City Council of the time. After undergoing a road-to-Damascus conversion, the Council authorised an excellent reinstatement of the Hall, competed in 1986.

The Music Hall, *the finest neoclassical building in Union Street. But are the banners really necessary? Their metal bands cannot be good for the pillars. Usually the portico is awash with sandwich boards, while posters and leaflets detract from the elegance of the interior.*

The Music Hall is the only survivor, narrowly, of a trio of fine Georgian buildings between South Silver Street and Huntly Street. The second building of the trio, No 198, a fine town house stood immediately to the west. No 198 was occupied for many years by Dr Robert Dyce, Professor of Midwifery at Marischal College and brother of the artist William Dyce. He was the son of the distinguished Dr William Dyce, but unlike his rather austere father was 'pleasant with an easy gentlemanly manner and a general favourite', as Ella Hill Burton Rodger wrote in her *Aberdeen Doctors* of 1893. A later resident was the inimitable Sir Alexander Anderson, Aberdeen's most entrepreneurial Lord Provost, but as early as the 1870s, No 198 became a YMCA, and so it remained until closure and demise. During the Second World War, Aberdeen ladies ran a popular canteen there, providing meals for soldiers unable to get home on leave.

Crimonmogate's House

The third building of this trio Crimonmogate's House, No 204 Union Street, dating from 1820 was the first building to go up west of Union Bridge, at the corner of the future Huntly Street. The Tuscan columns of its frontage were hand-polished and much admired. John Smith had designed it as a townhouse for Patrick Milne, who owned the estate of Crimonmogate in Buchan and had made his fortune trading with Peking, Bengal and Barbados. Behind his townhouse, on the future site of Crimon Place, he had a hothouse of exotic plants. On Milne's death, the estate was inherited by his cousin, Sir Charles Bannerman, and the Bannermans continued to live at Crimonmogate's House. It remained both their home and their business premises until 1874, when it was sold to the Royal Northern Club, which flitted here from the Lumsden house at No 1 Union Terrace. The RNC remained here until 1954, when it moved to Albyn Place.

In 1961, the Edinburgh development company had which attempted to demolish the Music Hall acquired Crimonmogate's House, along with the neighbouring YMCA, for demolition and redevelopment. Their demolition proposals invoked strong adverse reaction in Aberdeen. Part of an address given by the deputy managing director of the Edinburgh developers to reassure the Aberdeen Chamber of Commerce is worth quoting:

> Although they [Crimonmogate's House and the YMCA] were of possible historic interest, they had little else to commend. Architecturally they had little unity of relationship with the adjoining Music Hall building, but even so, when my company purchased the interests of both we insisted that careful consideration be given to the design of the proposed development. The new development will form a more effective architectural composition, both in relationship to the adjoining buildings and Union Street as a whole, than did the previous buildings.

One would hope that after speaking such blatant nonsense, the deputy managing director was taken out and shot, but one suspects he was greeted with a round of polite applause. The destruction of these buildings in 1963 was greeted with disbelief, angrily but fruitlessly opposed, and still regretted by those who remember them. Their replacement was described by the historian and journalist, Alexander Keith, as 'a cross between an upright garden frame and a broiler house'.

The modern retail development (after refurbishment) which replaced Crimonmogate's House. The Royal Insurance building to the left.

Huntly Street to Union Row

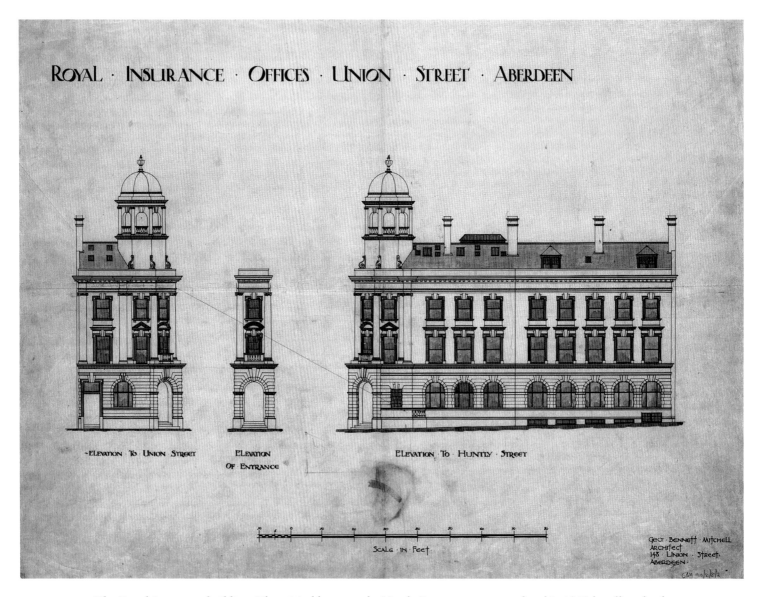

ROYAL · INSURANCE · OFFICES · UNION · STREET · ABERDEEN

ELEVATION · TO · UNION · STREET

ELEVATION
OF · ENTRANCE

ELEVATION · TO · HUNTLY · STREET

SCALE · IN · FEET

GEO · BENNETT · MITCHELL
ARCHITECT
143 · UNION · STREET ·
ABERDEEN

The Royal Insurance building. *The original house on the Huntly Street corner was replaced in 1910 by offices for the Royal Insurance Company at a cost of £20,000. The new building was designed in the style of a magnificent Venetian palazzo by George Bennett Mitchell, whose drawing is shown here. After Royal Insurance departed, the building stood empty for some time but eventually was handsomely restored. Starbucks coffee shop has been here since 2001.*

The 'Starbucks Row', Nos 212–20.

Continuing up the row, at Nos 212–6, left of Starbucks formerly Royal Insurance, were the Central Chambers, whose numerous occupants included George Watt & Stewart, architects, and W. Balfour Robb, advocates. In more recent years, No 214 has been the Paul & Williamson estate agency. Two storeys continue above the cornice, culminating in twin curving gablets, a junior version of those at No 154. The West End Academy used to be at No 216. It was opposite the house of Lachlan Mackinnon, who was a pupil there as an eight-year-old in the 1860s. John Marr had his pianoforte saloon at No 218 and Mackinnon reports that, 'the playground at the back abutted on to Marr's Piano Factory. The frequent breakage of glass in the factory by our balls and other missiles led to many complaints.'

In more recent times, shops at ground floor level included William Garden, gunsmith and fishing-tackle-maker, at No 216. The shop had such a fearsome array of weaponry in its front window that it was worth crossing the street just to take a look. A branch of the Royal Bank of Scotland is now located there, an original between the two giants. No 220 has a James & George Collie property shop at street level. Above cornice level, a splendid twentieth-century 'add on' rises a further two storeys, with an additional attic storey adorned with a balustrade and handsome 'broken' pediment, hiding a dormer. The entrance has changed, but No 220 in its higher reaches once housed a number of offices, including those of G H Bower & Gibb, advocates. G H was brother-in-law of the opera singer, Mary Garden, and one of the Bower brothers who were prominent in the business community. Herbert, the accountant, we have met already, across the road. The third brother, Haddon, was a principal of Bower & Florence, the Spital granite merchants.

The firm of G H Bower & Gibb was later headed by J Scott (Scotty) MacLachlan, a well known Tory councillor and Secretary of the Aberdeen Grammar School F. P. Club. In the 1950s, when lawyers worked on Saturday mornings, the G H Bower & Gibb Saturday morning staff conferences were held across at the Grill, so it is said. Another long standing law firm, Hunter & Gordon, was at No 222, formerly a townhouse of Patrick Bannerman, with the offices of John Rust, city architect, next door at No 224. Some years ago, the ground floor was transformed into the Nile, a pub with an Egyptian theme, featuring murals by a local painter. This has since become Stadia, a pub specialising, as its name suggests, in TV sports coverage. It was disappointing to see the Nile murals go. Nos 222–4 is the only building in Union Street to retain its railings, steps and open basement.

The apparently unassuming No 226, right of the Skipton building, had been a North of Scotland Bank and, after amalgamation, a Clydesdale Bank. It is currently a branch of Lloyds TSB. Probably once a townhouse, it has a tiny entrance porch, pretending to be a portico, where Ionic columns, their volutes almost dancing a jig, and pilasters squeeze in together. The twin door knobs have lions' heads and the metal, art nouveau fanlight resembles a thick spider's web. Finally to the end piece of the row, the good-looking No 230, the Skipton Building Society office. The ground floor has been acceptably modernised and it makes a neat turn into Union Row to link up with the timeless Investment House.

Small but grand. *The entrance to the Lloyds TSB bank at No 226 Union Street.*

Skipton to Starbucks. *Looking east, from the Skipton building back to Starbucks, a terrace whose original houses dated from around 1840. In the centre, Nos 222–4, Stadia, is the only building in Union Street to retain its railings, steps and open basement. The 'apparently unassuming' No 226 is between Stadia and the Skipton building.*

An aerial photograph *of the section under discussion, delineated by two church buildings, Soul, formerly the Langstane Kirk, on the right side, and Gilcomston South Church to the left, with Union Street cutting through in the centre. In the foreground long buildings run between the south side of Union Street and Langstane Place. Dominating the shot, however, is the striking Union Plaza in Union Row. Completed by Stewart Milne Developments in 2008, at a cost of over £25 million, this ultra-modern office development has attracted as tenants, leading legal and financial firms such as Paul & Williamson and Aberdeen Asset Management. It should bring new life to the west end of Union Street. Coincidentally, the Plaza towers directly above Amicable House, the great Aberdeen office development of the 1930s.*

CHAPTER SEVEN

FROM THE FREE WEST* TO GILCOMSTON SOUTH

ART DECO AND AUTOMOBILES

'Ye citizens of Aberdeen,
Nae wonder that ye glower.
They hae closed anither picter hoose,
The Majestic's days are ower.'

'Cinemas', Scotland the What?

We have arrived at the final stretch of Union Street West, the end of Union Street – or the beginning, depending on which direction one was heading – at least before 1890. This was the western plain, once covered with whins and broom which had to be brought in from nature. According to George Walker in *Aberdeen Awa'*, the only grumbler was a Mr Beggrie, who had already reclaimed ground from Little Chapel Street in the north across to Langstane Place in the south and turned it into a small public park:

> It was the general resort of the citizens in summer for curds and cream and strawberries; while every Saturday for the small charge of twopence, boys were allowed to eat any quantity of gooseberries they could gorge … It was the general trysting place for budding sweethearts.

Beggrie's pleasure garden had to go, to make way for the great road which would run across it.

The Bon Accord Street Corner
Before setting off along the south side, have a look at this splendid photo overleaf of a motorcycle club rally taken at the junction of Union Street and Bon Accord Street. It indicates several aspects of Aberdeen life around 1912. Why, for example, is the start being held near the top of Bon Accord Street? Partly because there was plenty of space where the street opened out, almost forming a square, correcting an early misalignment with the

* *Later the Langstane Kirk and now Soul.*

The start of a motorcycle club rally *of around 1912, near the junction of Union Street and Bon Accord Street.*

Hardgate/Langstane Place. But the earliest motorcycle dealers had already set up shop in the stretch of Union Street between Bon Accord Street and Bon Accord Terrace, with rear access from Langstane Place. This is where the bikers would want to be. Quite a number of the men are wearing not only the obligatory caps with goggles but the current version of 'leathers'. The women wear hats tied down with scarves. Ladies' motoring apparel was being advertised by Pratt & Keith, Millets and Watt & Grant at this time.

Behind the motorcyclists, on the other side of Union Street, is a rare view of No 232, the tall townhouse of Dr Angus Fraser. Dominating the middle ground is the east side of a prominent city kirk, the West United Free Church as it then was, now Soul, a café-bar. At the left is Nos 10–14 Bon Accord Street, an agricultural-looking building with a cart entrance that would have been quite at home in one of the larger fairm toons. It was the workplace of 'John Blaikie & Sons, plumbers, braziers, (to His Majesty King George V) bell and brass founders, electrical engineers, gasfitters, coppersmiths etc.'.

The elegant front of Jackson's Garage. The curving turn into Langstane Place can just be glimpsed at the right. It replaced Blackie's agricultural-style premises.

John Jackson, motor car engineer, left his North Silver Street garage in the mid-1920s to take over the former Blaikie premises. By the early 1930s, he had also become an 'agent'. In a year or two he specifically represented Bedford and Vauxhall. Presently a magnificent garage, with A G R Mackenzie, son of Marshall, as architect, appeared on the old Blaikie site, a handsome, almost geometric piece with art deco details. The central portion is impressively cool, with long, narrow windows, 1930s-style clock, and a winged logo bearing the date 1937 and the initial J for Jackson. Just visible is a ramp, extreme left, which spiralled round the interior, allowing cars to be driven up to the roof and parked there. The idea came from Campbell's livery stables and posting house across the road, where the distinctive inner courtyard was encircled by galleries. The horses were led up a ramp, which rose to two levels, giving access to their loose boxes. The stables later became Campbell's Motor Services and after a long period of desuetude, were replaced by the Galleria shopping centre. Across the road, SMT succeeded Jackson in the 1950s. The premises are now occupied by Slater Menswear.

The South Side: From Bon Accord Street to Bon Accord Terrace

And now to Union Street and the Bon Accord Street/Bon Accord Terrace row, built between 1820 and 1840. The houses with long gardens running back to the Hardgate (as Langstane Place then was) had the usual West End mix of gentry, doctors, advocates and the odd merchant. Dr William Williamson was practising medicine at the once isolated Bon Accord Street corner house, while John and Anthony Blaikie, advocates, were a few doors further along, sharing the building with Alex Stronach, writer, a less elevated form of solicitor.

The Blaikies caused a sensation in 1862. Their firm was sequestrated with liabilities of between £200,000 and £300,000, a sum amounting to millions in today's terms. They are said to have fled the country. West of the Blaikies we find Miss Innes, Henry Lumsden of Auchindoir, Dr William Keith, Mr Farquhar of Johnston Lodge and, near the end, the home of the Hogarths, Aberdeen's leading food-preservers, who had a factory in College Street. John Duncan, advocate, is at the last house before Bon Accord Row, later Bon Accord Terrace.

By 1865, Dr William Williamson had died and his tall house with its garden on the corner and the adjoining feu to the west were bought by the Free West Church. After several adventures, and with some money in its pocket, the church had decided that the Union Street/Bon Accord corner would make a fine and commanding site for a new kirk. James

Soul, *the fifth name for this former church.*

Matthews, architect, had drawn up the plans. Williamson's house was demolished but the front garden survived. When the new Free West opened here in 1869, it was one of the most magnificent ecclesiastical buildings in the city. The building cost £2300, had seating for 1050, a handsome interior, a magnificent 175-foot spire and a rose window. This was probably the first Free Kirk stained-glass window in Aberdeen, and it gave rise to some sniping from co-religionists, 'as savouring of popery'. The sandstone spire caused problems of a material kind, for it eroded over the years, as Pratt & Keith knew to their cost. The Free West had fine ministers, but none greater than the first, Dr Dyce Davidson, described in J. Ogilvie Skea's *The Free West* (1963) as, 'a man of unruffled sweetness of character, a preacher of impressive power and a minister of rare faithfulness and devotion'. There is a portrait of him, a man with the look of a visionary, by John 'Spanish' Philip.

By 1903, most of the terrace of original houses that adjoined the kirk had been converted into shops. Their railings, beloved of Provost Leys, had been removed and the building line moved back to create a wider pavement. Outside the kirk, Dr Williamson's former front garden had been grassed over and was left protruding beyond the building line. The Town Council, wishing to purchase the offending seventy-six square yards and 'even up' the area, entered into negotiations with the General Assembly of the Church of Scotland. These took six years to come to fruition, but eventually the price was fixed at £38, £18 more than the Town had originally offered. The Free West, which, as a result of church amalgamations became the West United Free, the West Church of St Andrew and latterly, the Langstane Kirk, was left with a small forecourt, a lively place where there was an annual art show and books sales on a Saturday morning for church funds. The Langstane Kirk played a positive, ecumenical role in the city centre, but unfortunately, in spite of members' determination to keep the kirk open, the congregation was dissolved in 1999 by edict of the Church of Scotland. The building at present is Soul, a café bar with casino, which has been thoughtfully converted. It is worth going in, even if only to view the stunning stained-glass windows created between 1937 and 1953 by John M Aiken, a head of Gray's School of Art, to designs by the architect George Bennett Mitchell, devoted elder and Sunday school teacher there.

For many years, this stretch of Union Street was a cyclists' Mecca. By the beginning of the twentieth century, No 337 – next but one to the kirk, and formerly Mrs Graham's townhouse – had become the Caledonian Motor Car and Cycle Co. Meanwhile, the Rossleigh Cycle & Motor Co. had arrived along at No 383. The Caledonian was succeeded at No 337 by the Raleigh Cycle Co. About 1910, this was joined next door at No 339 by Rudge–Whitworth

Part of the Bon Accord Street-Bon Accord *Terrace stretch. Above the gleaming coach, a glimpse of the spire of what is now Soul, helps one get one's bearings. The house railings on the south side have vanished while a few remain on the north. Some shops have appeared, among them cycle shops. Early in the twentieth century the West End of Union Street was the place to buy a bike as well as to learn to ride one, judging by this photo.*

Cycles. Alexanders, cycle, motor and radio dealers replaced Rudge–Whitworth at No 339 about 1917. During the First World War, Raleigh went to No 345 and in the 1920s D C Cruickshank, cycle and motorcycle specialist, arrived at No 347. An enjoyable pastime of my childhood was to walk from Ferryhill through to Union Street to inspect the cycle shops. Eventually, I saved up ten guineas, checking every week that my favourite was still in stock during a long nail-biting time, and eventually made the momentous purchase of my first bike, from D C Cruickshank. It lasted for over thirty years.

It was always a thrill to see some magnificent model sitting in the plate-glass window of Rossleigh's, agents for Rover & Jaguar. The first to arrive in Union Street, Rossleigh's was the last of the old brigade to go, around 1970, though Halfords, the cycle shop, deserves a mention, upholding the tradition in the modern era. Some shops in this stretch extended back to Langstane Place, hence their popularity with the car, bike and motorcycle trade. Vehicles were taken through from wide entrances at the back to be displayed in the shop front. Substantial space for storage and workshops was also available, necessary to cabinetmakers and furniture shops.

By the late 1880s, Galloway & Sykes, one of three well-known local furniture shops, had moved into No 365. They were cabinetmakers, upholsterers, billiard-table-makers and coffin-makers. The other furniture shops were J & A Ogilvie, which was at No 369 by 1904, and Roberts – lacking, like Inspector Morse, a Christian name – at No 419. All were local men. Ogilvie's fitted out the 'state of the art' Aberdeen cinemas in the 1930s, and put out a series of patriotic adverts during the Second World War: 'This Third Wartime Christmas finds us still carrying on and doing our best in very difficult times.' The firm was later acquired by Hugh Fraser's Wylie & Lochhead.

Other memorable shops of the past include Miss Mary Silver's millinery and knitwear shop, which sat beside the kirk for many years, and Wilson of Belfast's linen shop, next door at a later date. J & C Graham's shoe shop was at No 389 and an early branch of Jaeger was at No 391. Worthy of a mention too is the double shop, stylish but short-lived, at Nos 339–345. In 1906 – before it became Rudge or Raleigh or Alexanders – it was the premises of W. Mitchell, ladies' tailor and outfitter, who sold 'The Best of Everything at Moderate Prices'.

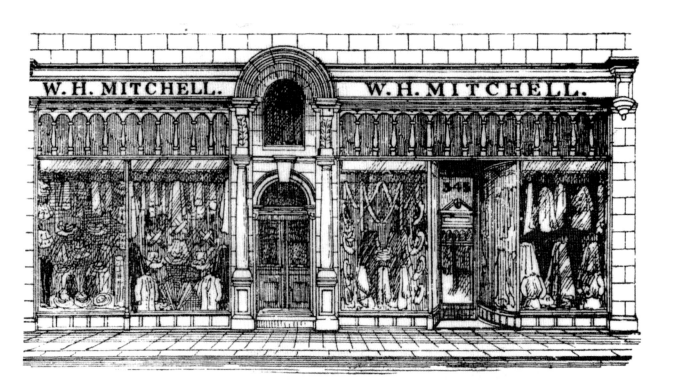

Above, the stylish double shop of W H Mitchell, drawn in 1906 and below, the same shop(s) at time of writing. *High and Mighty is at No 339, and Jaeger at No 345, once the premises of Lumsden & Gibson, Italian warehousemen. The door between them, No 343, is one of the handsomest in Union Street. Yu, a Chinese restaurant, is right of Jaeger.*

The Milkmaid, *once D C Cruikshank's cycle shop and currently Yu. The cycle racks were through at the back where the Milkmaid restaurant can be glimpsed.*

The same area as shown in the cyclists' photo *and another of these Aberdeen on a flag day shots! The terrace of buildings on the south side, right, runs unbroken from Soul to La Tasca, a restaurant with a fascia that is colourful, yet appropriate to the building. The former Refuge Assurance Company's building extreme right, breaks the terrace. Bruce Miller's clock in the centre of the row is a welcome addition to the townscape. The north side, left, was home to a number of the city's leading physicians. The bulk, tiny windows and massive canopy of Caledonian House can be made out opposite the church, where the Majestic once stood. The NatWest Bank is extreme left.*

Some years ago, the long-established, family-owned music shop, Bruce Millers, moved from its Loch Street and Holburn Street shops into the former Galloway & Sykes property, No 365, combining all its ranges under one roof. While remaining true to its roots, selling a wide range of instruments and running music classes, Bruce Millers continued to expand, selling radios, televisions, CDs and DVDs, all sorts of high-tech equipment, newspapers and magazines and sandwiches. The premises also houses a popular coffee shop which looks out onto Langstane Place. It had a good book department, specialising in local publications, but unfortunately this has been discontinued.

Bruce Miller's frontage *with a scintillating window display of musical instruments, and the musical clock above.*

The Refuge Assurance building with, left, William Brown & Sons, cabinetmakers, soon after their arrival at No 373 in the 1920s. The firm was later taken over by their neighbours, J & A Ogilvie. Right, a group of schoolchildren pours into James E Henderson, Kodak specialists, at No 377.

In 1901, the Refuge Assurance Company commissioned Nos 373–7 from the architect John Rust – his office was across the road – and for once he seems to have lost his lightsome touch. Here are great canted bays, heavy mullions and pedimented windows. The attic storey with its mini Corinthian colonettes (wee columns) and occulus (wee round window) looks as if it belonged somewhere else, like Versailles. Perhaps Rust, who was also the city architect, as John Smith had been, was overwhelmed by the importance of designing for Union Street.

The Refuge occupied the first floor. From the 1930s, James E Henderson, the photographic and ciné specialist, was at No 377 with a massive brass 'Kodak' in the front window, something of a landmark. The shop later moved to Rose Street. Today Nos 373–7 offer us Toni & Guy, hairdressers, and Careers Scotland. The careers office also has a part of the neighbouring premises designed by Archibald Simpson, in toto Nos 381–91, and has tried to marry the totally different buildings with obtrusive signage, virtually obliterating their frontages.

The former Refuge building in 2008. *Careers Scotland tenant its west half as well as the very different east half of the neighbouring building by Archibald Simpson.*

Chivas Brothers, grocers, 1969. This building was an Archibald Simpson foray into Union Street West. It was previously Rossleigh's and is now Michie's.

This is the west part of the same Archibald Simpson building, once home to Rossleigh motors, with a stylish façade and a canopy that actually adds something. Our photo dates from 1969 when Chivas Brothers of whisky fame, royal warrant holders, were in residence. The grocers' shop and delicatessen were on the ground floor and an excellent restaurant was upstairs, with the entrance on the left. Chivas were attracted by the great length of the premises. Here they had space to combine the 'backshop' work of the grocery retail business – they had previously run a branch at 501 Union Street – with whisky distribution formerly carried out at their King Street depot. These activities took place in what is now Michie's gift department. Unfortunately Chivas had to move when the new 'artic' lorries found it impossible to negotiate Langstane Place. Michie's the chemist then acquired the building. Like Bruce Millers, Michie's has retained its core business, and expanded to become a popular small department store, with gifts, stationery, all sorts of specialties and a coffee shop.

Finally, shown opposite, at the corner with Bon Accord Terrace, are Nos 393–9. This building dates from around 1830, predating the neighbouring Simpson building, and is thought to be by John Smith. This is a fine and timeless building. Between the late 1860s and the 1880s it was the home of John Forbes White, grain merchant, the miller of Kettock's Mill on the Don. White was a true lad o' pairts: first bursar at Marischal College, a Greek scholar, a connoisseur of the arts and a considerable benefactor of the new Aberdeen Art Gallery. In the 1860s, White had a chance meeting on a train with the up-and-coming artist, Daniel Cottier, a Glaswegian of Manx extraction. Before the journey was over, White had persuaded Cottier to come to Aberdeen and work on a number of commissions. These were mainly in Old Aberdeen, but included creating a picture gallery at the back of his Union Street townhouse, on the Bon Accord Terrace corner. The miller had chosen his unknown interior decorator well. Cottier later moved to London and by 1873 had opened for business in New York, specialising in the decorative arts, particularly stained-glass. He was a major influence on L C Tiffany, creator of the famous lamps.

John Smith's timeless building, left, formerly Halifax House, stands four-square at the end of Union Street West. The former George Hotel in Bon Accord Terrace, now in a poor state, is glimpsed at the centre. Jimmy Chung's buffet is at the right. The expansive plate-glass window looks uncomfortably high for the building.

At a later date and for many years this was the premises of the Halifax Building Society now, of course, amalgamated with the Bank of Scotland. Their office was at No 399 and at No 395 were the legendary Fullers, confectioners, whose tea room at the spacious rear was, as I seem to recall, down a few steps. Their dainty cakes, wrapped in cellophane paper, I remember well. Today, the building is occupied by Northern Rock and the property shop of solicitors Raeburn, Christie, Clark & Wallace.

The North Side: From Union Row to Summer Street

From its earliest days, this side of the road was patronised by the most distinguished members of Aberdeen's medical profession. Angus Fraser, MD, LLD whose house at No 232 is visible in the 'bikers' rally' photo was Senior Lecturer in Clinical Medicine at Aberdeen University and an Assessor on the University Court. At No 248 was Surgeon Lieutenant-Colonel Charles MacQuibban. Rudolph A Galloway, MD was at No 250, with Professor Sir Alexander Ogston at No 252 and George Williamson, MD at No 256.

One is tempted to say that when the architect Tommy Scott Sutherland appeared on the scene they all scattered, but in truth, most were gone before the human dynamo arrived. As early as 1911, Angus Fraser's corner house had been demolished and replaced by a very handsome Clydesdale Bank. Next door at No 234 was La Scala, Aberdeen's first custom–built cinema. Dating from 1914 it had a tea terrace, which permitted tea to be taken while watching the film, a full-scale orchestra, and its own generator in the basement, which my father remembered producing a sinister noise.

By the 1930s the entrepreneurial architect, T Scott Sutherland started to colonise this row, acquiring the home of the great surgeon, Sir Alexander Ogston at No 252, one of the last private residences in Union Street. It was here while experimenting 'in a small laboratory built behind my dwelling house' in 1881 that Ogston made his celebrated discovery of *Staphylococcum*, the pus organism, a discovery that eventually led to far fewer fatalities after surgery. Tommy's plans to turn No 252 into an indoor midget golf course failed to materialise before the craze passed. The Scottish Amicable Building Society then entered the scene, proposing to make an offer for No 252, provided Sutherland could acquire for them No 250, home of the last doctor, R A Galloway, now retired. Both houses would then be demolished and replaced by a magnificent new building, Amicable House, to be designed by Sutherland. Dr Galloway was unwilling to sell until Tommy took him down to the basement and confronted him with some dry rot. That settled it. Nos 250 and 252 were acquired for the building society at a cost of £1,400 and demolished. Amicable House arose in their place in 1934, a custom-built office block in art deco style inside and out, costing £16,000. Sutherland's own office was based here, so everything had to be of the best, with no out-of-date magazines in the waiting areas. There were three floors of offices, and two flats above, with three shops at pavement level. George Sim, furrier, Hector Powe, tailor, and Roderick Tweedie, who sold county-style ladies' clothes, were tenants almost from the start.

Amicable House in the early 21st century.

At much the same time, Tommy Sutherland also designed the powerful Majestic cinema just to the east, replacing La Scala, and 'quite dwarfing' even Amicable House. It was another essay in art deco, built from Kemnay granite. He regarded it as his finest design. It cost £45,000 and was hailed at that time as the boldest concept in cinema design in Scotland. All the work was carried out by local tradesmen, including the carpeting, the decor and the magical lighting, forever changing.

The Majestic and its neighbours, 1972. *From the left: Gilcomston South Church, marking the end of this stretch, Amicable House flying the flag, a surviving original house (now offices), the Majestic and the fine Clydesdale Bank which replaced Dr Angus Fraser's house.*

Repairs underway at Caledonian House, *which replaced the Majestic and the Clydesdale Bank. Amicable House is at the far left, then an original house/office. The conglomeration of street 'furniture' outside this building, the narrowness of the pavement and the gloomy canopy above make it an area to be avoided.*

Aberdeen Motors, 1959. *Claud Hamilton's successor at No 254 Union Street shows off the new Mini. The bar that now occupies this building is appropriately called* The Filling Station.

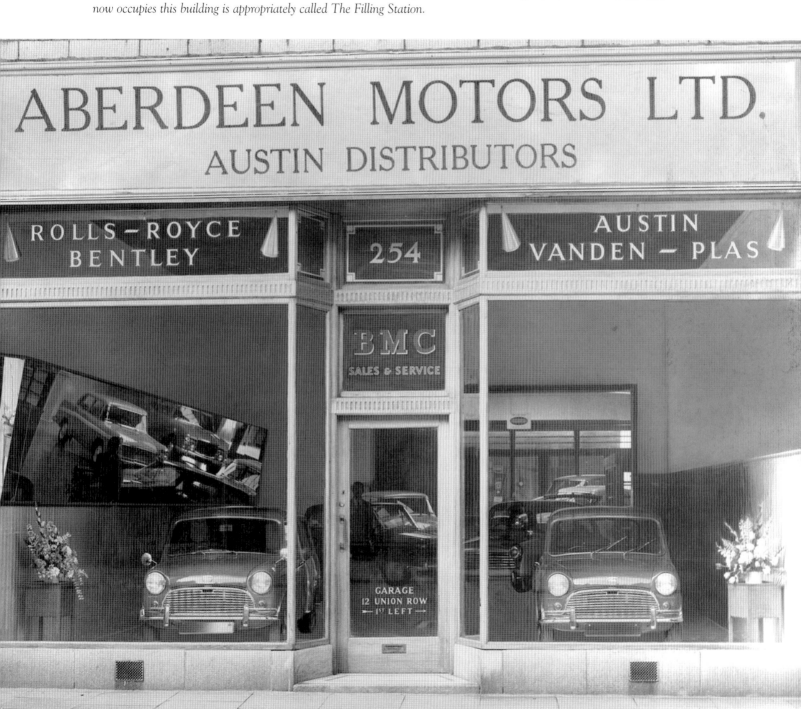

In Silver Screen in the Silver City (1988) Michael Thomson writes of the Majestic:

> It effectively demonstrated Sutherland's talent for using granite in simple shapes to produce something that was unmistakeably of its time, yet possessing a distinctive local flavour.

Shades of the technique of Smith and Simpson. Owned by a new company, Caledonian Theatres, the Majestic, opened in 1936. By 1938, James F Donald's Aberdeen Cinemas had acquired a major interest. Though the doctors had gone and only a couple of original buildings remained, this row had style. The Majestic, with Amicable House and Jackson's Garage across in Bon Accord Street, formed a little art deco pocket.

The Majestic closed in 1974, and was later demolished along with its handsome smaller neighbour, the Clydesdale Bank of 1911. A great pity. They were succeeded by Caledonian House, an unprepossessing lump of an office block with an outsize canopy which drips on passers-by from time to time, and a grid of numerous small windows offering a hint of penal servitude. It housed Aberdeen's first Waterstone's at ground-floor level, which has now been replaced by a charity furniture shop, with a delicatessen on the Union Row corner.

Speaking of Union Row, it was a popular address for coach-builders like Robert Ness and his successors R & J Shinnie, renowned builders of tram bodies. Claud Hamilton, motor engineer, was based at No 254 Union Street from the beginning of the twentieth century and, like the car and motorcycle dealers of Union Street/Langstane Place, made use of back-to-back premises in Union Row to bring cars into the showroom.

Aberdeen Motors, which survived until 1973, was set up by a group of Aberdeen businessmen to provide work for First World War veterans, and was originally based at small and modest premises in Huntly Street. This takes us to Gilcomston South Church on the Summer Street/Union Street junction, neither small nor modest, but large and imposing. It had its origins in that famous Chapel of Ease at the far end of Summer Street which became Gilcomston Parish Church. At the Disruption, the great schism in the Church of Scotland in 1843, most of the congregation came 'out' and built their first Gilcomston Free Kirk, that very hall in Huntly Street, later home to Aberdeen Motors.

By the 1850s, the minister of Gilcomston Free was a Revd Dr Walter Macgilvray, of whom Alexander Gammie writes:

> He became famous as an antagonist of Roman Catholicism, and his great anti-popery discourses, in which he let himself go in great bursts of passion, made something of a sensation and became the talk of the town.

Macgilvray's congregation grew immensely as a result of this entertainment. The modest Huntly Street Kirk was filled to overflowing and a large, new church became essential. The site chosen, until recently a cornfield, was at the junction with Summer Street. William Smith was the architect and the church opened in 1868. Doubtless the Catholics were glad to see the back of the Revd Macgilvray. Their new cathedral, St Mary's, Huntly Street, was being built at this time, a stone's throw from Old Gilcomston Free, the Huntly Street Hall. St Mary's, arising stone by stone before his very eyes, may have fuelled Macgilvray's vitriolic forays.

Gilcomston South Kirk (previously Gilcomston Free) is one of Union Street's great landmarks, with its vivid polychromatic details, dazzling new spire, wheel window and massed gables to Summer Street. There is even a 'minaret', though no muezzin appears to call one to prayers – at least not so far. By the early 1990s, the sandstone spire was in a dangerous state, but was dismantled and rebuilt with substantial funding from numerous bodies. The situation was touch-and-go for a time, but Union Street's historic skyline was eventually preserved. Gilcomston's Wayside Pulpit adds a touch of spirituality to a largely hedonistic street.

No 343. One of the most handsome entrances in Union Street

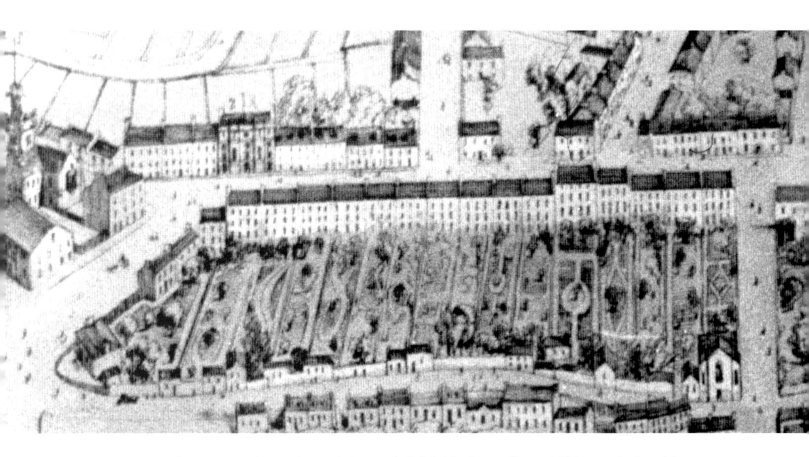

Union Place, 1850. *Its long gardens reach down to the little holiday homes of Justice Mill Lane at the foot of the picture. The white church, bottom right, once Holburn Free, became Charley's night club. Right of Charley's, Bon Accord Terrace leads up to the Union Street/Union Place junction. On the other side, extreme right, Summer Street, being older, was the original demarcation line, the end of Union Street. Left of Summer Street are Chapel Street then Rose Street, both running north. Left of Rose Street, the tall dark building is the Waterhouse, later a bank. Extreme left on the island site is the Free Church College, later Christ's College, now a night club. Babbie (Barbara) Law's shop is in the building in front of it, right. A detail from George Washington Wilson's Bird's Eye View.*

CHAPTER EIGHT

UNION PLACE

'Although it was in 1885 that Babbie Law disposed of the licensed shop wherein the carters of granite setts from Rubislaw were wont to quench their thirst, the corner still goes by her name.'

A Thousand Years of Aberdeen, Alexander Keith, 1972

Union Place: Bon Accord Terrace to Holburn Street and Summer Street to Alford Place

From early in the nineteenth century this area was known as Union Place. Before that it was the Damhead Road. It was incorporated into Union Street by 1890, when the town was having one of its periodic bouts of 'reddin' up'. Each side of the road has a different origin. As far as the south is concerned, the historian William Robbie recalled in *Aberdeen: Its Traditions and History* (1893) that a few houses had been built on what is now Justice Mill Lane, south facing, looking over the Ferryhill Valley. 'They were considered quite in the country,' writes Robbie, 'and were used mainly as summer cottages, their owners preferring their more confined but perhaps cosier apartments in the town during the winter months.' When the development of Union Place, or at least the western plain, of which it is part, went ahead as originally suggested by the surveyor Abercrombie, building plots were laid out to bring in much-needed cash by selling feus. The south side was laid out along the edge of the long back gardens of the holiday homes. Some of the houses built there remain, much altered, disguised as business premises.

The developers of Union Place did not have to follow the rigorous conditions demanded of their Union Street counterparts. Even so, the Union Place feu charters were strict enough to prevent the street from being unduly narrowed by indiscriminate building. Union Street was seventy feet wide and at Union Place the width was reduced by ten feet. It does not seem to have been quite as gentrified as Union Street West; nevertheless, in 1855 the south side was occupied by W A Skene of Lethenty, Mrs Stuart of Laithers, Professor David Gray, Mrs Rodger, Mrs Leslie of Memsie and Miss Dingwall Fordyce; while residents of the north side included the Misses Shand, Mrs Walker late of Wester Fintry and Miss Still of Millden. There were also four solicitors, three doctors, a pharmacist, two mill owners and two grocers.

The west end of Union Place, better known as Babbie Law's.
Babbie Law's shop, with rounded end, is to the left of Christ's College, centre, top, but the friendly-sounding name was given to the area around it, before 'Holburn Junction' was ever heard of. The Waterhouse is at the extreme right. Next to it, with cart outside, is a two-storey house, later No 492 Union Street, with steps, railings and sunks. Beyond is a little terrace of houses. Miss Warrack's Boarding School, later Albyn School for Girls, was based in this terrace at No 52 Union Place, from 1869 until 1886, incorporating No 53 from 1874. Railings and sunks prevail on the south side, left. Someone has a nice entrance porch behind the men in white. The Playhouse was later built at the extreme left.

A chromolithograph of Union Place, late 1880s. At the top, Babbie Law's has been replaced by a bank building, now a branch of Lloyds TSB. The railings are going and some new buildings have appeared. Front left, a woman, perhaps a servant, is out shopping. Opposite, to the left of the Waterhouse, a grand, four-storey tenemental building has taken over the eastern half of the little terrace. It includes ground-floor shops, complete with awnings. Perhaps Miss Warrack moved her school to No 6 Albyn Place at this time.

In 1889–90, the last entry in the street directory before Union Place became part of Union Street, shows considerable changes since 1855. Every building had an entry, judging by the unbroken run of street numbers. Numerous trades and professions are represented, including three doctors and a lawyer, William McKinnon, stockbroker, the British Linen Bank, William Cay, funeral undertaker, a dentist, a chemist, a teacher, teachers of music and dancing, confectioners, five dressmakers and outfitters, two milliners and a berlin wool dealer, a game dealer and a butcher, two dairies, two fruiterers and two grocers, a music-seller, stationer, tobacconist, two watchmakers a plumber, two shoemakers, two bakers, one of whom is Mitchell & Muil and two fruiterers.

Edmund Geering, a former apprentice of George Washington Wilson, had his studio at No 10, later No 416 Union Street. The gentry appear to have given up their plain old houses. Perhaps they were moving to the Rubislaw Den and other West End areas being developed in some style at this time, by the Aberdeen Land Association and various noted architects. Consequently, the tradesmen and shopkeepers were serving such customers beyond Union Place, whose domestic buildings were being gradually transformed into commercial enterprises.

The South Side: From Bon Accord Terrace to Holburn Street

Another Aberdeen flag day. On the south side, left, is Jimmy Chung's, on the corner of Bon Accord Terrace. On the north side, right, Summer Street is just out of range.

Is anything left of the original Union Place on the south side? There are patches of terracing, from Bon Accord Terrace corner to the former Capitol ensemble. No 401 on the corner was for years a grocer's, then a popular branch of Boots, with a branch of Pullars of Perth, dry cleaners, next door. A later occupant was Cupids, a pub with a façade dominated by yellow imitation arches. Barney Rubble's and a Long Island Iced Tea place followed. At this time a plate-glass window was inserted, too high for the height of the building. Now Jimmy Chung's popular Chinese buffet occupies the corner building, the basement restaurant reaching under what was once the George Hotel in Bon Accord Terrace, a favourite howff with a good restaurant, the Langstane Room, in the 1950s and 1960s. The George was converted into flats years ago, but now looks utterly desolate. Next to Jimmy Chung's, the Cut Above, Saks hairdressers and Pure menswear form an attractive, co-ordinated unit.

Saks and Pure were preceded, years earlier, by Miss Nicoll, milliner, and Miss Gerard, jeweller and silversmith. The two shops sat side by side for over half a century. Miss Isabella Nicoll arrived at No 409 Union Street in 1911. She was, by that time, thirty-three years of age and had made the move from King Street, continuing to specialise in 'New and Exclusive Designs; Wedding and Mourning Orders a Speciality'. By the time of the First World War, the shop had become simply Nicoll, though my mother and aunt never referred to it as anything other than 'Miss Nicoll's'. Next door at No 411, Miss Gerard, who produced fine silverwork, had already become 'M'.

Miss Nicoll's husband, James F. Gordon, may also have had a hand in the change. Jimmy, recalled as a charming and elegant figure who always wore a buttonhole, started off in his father's shoemaking business in Broad Street, became a book-keeper, then devoted himself to running his wife's shop, and continued to do so after her death in 1935. Nicoll was still there in the 1960s, though by that time M. Gerard had been succeeded by the jeweller, Norman Primrose.

*A **tall trio**. From left, Aberdein Considine, a dilapidated former Roberts' furniture shop and the Justice Mill pub.*

*A **splendid window display** at M Gerard, the Union Street jeweller.*

Aberdein Considine's property shop at No 415 has the best-kept parking area round in Justice Mill Lane. The immortal William Cay, undertaker, who had been in the area for 100 years (at least) according to his advertisements, was a predecessor here and the same funereal vase decorated the window, year in, year out. The shop subsequently became the more cheerful June (Deeside), with several floors of china on display. Like its neighbours to the east, No 415 is a Union Place original. It is the same height, but pedimented dormers give an impression of even greater height.

The next two buildings, the first empty and the second occupied by The Justice Mill, are possible originals. If you consult the Bird's Eye View (page 164), you'll see the first three from Bon Accord Terrace at the usual level, then the next group shooting up. The empty shop, No 419, with the unusual Venetian window at first-floor level, was once Roberts (Aberdeen) Ltd, one of the area's famous furniture shops. Sports shops followed, and a basement nightclub, none of which succeeded. The Justice Mill, at No 423, is a pub rather than a mill, but at least is trying to show a rapport with local history. The Sixty Minute Cleaners operated from these premises for years, using the great depth at the back to carry out the bulk of the dry-cleaning.

Next came the Arcade at No 11a Union Place (Nos 431–3 Union Street from 1890) but this vanished long ago. Built as a market to replace the burnt out New Market, it failed. It was too remote from the east end of Union Street, and in any case, the New Market was quickly rebuilt. It then housed a variety of enterprises, shops, the Arcade Rink, and the Arcade Motor Garage from around 1905 until 1910. By 1910, the Arcade had been transformed, under H Bannister Howard, as the Electric Theatre – 'Every Seat will be a Tip-up, Nicely Cushioned'. Howard was the first to introduce continuous performance, with tea, cakes and newspapers in a room adjoining the auditorium. The cinema historian Michael Thomson reports that the Electric was so popular that Howard was able to persuade trams to stop at the Arcade entrance.

After the First World War, the Electric was acquired by Aberdeen's oldest established cinema circuit, Aberdeen Picture Places. The new owners announced plans to build a 'large, up-to-date cinema' on the site. The result, of course, was the Capitol, mostly designed by the architect A G R Mackenzie. It opened in 1933 and was Aberdeen's most perfect cinema. It had art deco detailing inside and out, where stainless-steel semi-circular hand plates formed full circles when the front doors were closed. Useful yet handsome – Archibald Simpson would have approved of them – though it's anyone's guess what he would have made of F Rowland Tims, thundering up on his Compton theatre organ belting out the Prelude to

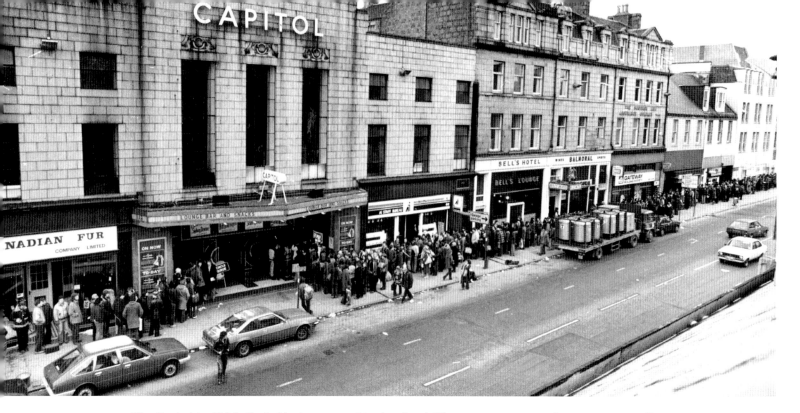

The Capitol in 1980, flanked by its two matching 'pavilions'. The massive queues are for a pop concert. Beer is being piped down to the cellars of the Balmoral Bar, part of Bell's Hotel, the large building behind the lorry. Stepping over the pipe was a hazard while walking down Union Street. The pavement was cracked, but the critical area is now paved with synthetic cassies, perhaps reinforced! Next to the Bell's building, right, are two reconstructed original houses, and extreme right, Holburn House which replaced the Playhouse and James Scott, the fireplace specialists.

Act Three of *Lohengrin*. (The legendary Tims also served as organist at both the Langstane Kirk and Gilcomston South). Few pleasures were greater than having high tea at the Capitol Restaurant with its long, elegant windows, served by waitresses dressed like waitresses, followed by a visit to the beautifully appointed Ladies' Room, then across, or downstairs to watch a film. All gone, alas. When cinemas were closing everywhere, the Capitol kept bailing out for a time, presenting live shows in the 1950s, and its first pop concert in 1961. The café became a bar.

The Capitol was eventually purchased by the leisure group Luminar, and in 2003 split horizontally to form two 'brand-name' nightclubs. The Capitol building was Category B-listed in 1976, rare for a cinema, with special mention of its 'restrained art-deco interior', though little good that has done. A local publication commented in 2004 that the Union Street frontage 'has been in an inexplicably shabby and neglected condition for months past'. Little has changed. The Capitol ensemble included two 'pavilion' wings, for years, occupied by the somewhat formidable Canadian Fur Company on the east and William Munro, the well-known fruiterer on the west. Both vanished years ago and the sense of uniformity has been lost.

Bell's Hotel, immediately west of the Capitol group though now closed, provided good homely fare. It was accessed by the central door and the stairs. Harold F. Bell, 'genial and flamboyant', as Archibald Hopkin described him in *The Aberdeen Pub Companion* (1975), another Union Street gent who sported a buttonhole, acquired the premises in 1965, gave the place a face lift, and established it as a favourite city watering-hole. There are two ground-floor bars here, both places for serious drinking, and handy, given the proximity of the bookies, to celebrate a win or drown one's sorrows. Though the frosted glass in their windows is attractive and the upper storeys are not without character, the bars resemble an abandoned poorhouse at the moment.

Redevelopment is planned, making use of the vast space at the rear in Justice Mill Lane. Remax AAA have the rest of the building.

Approaching Holburn Junction, early 1970s. *At the extreme left are two buildings, tatty here, but seen after refurbishment, right, in the previous photo. At the left, Marlowe the hairdresser is at No 465. It has only half a frontage, but is set back to create an illusion of space. The frontage was at odds with the more utilitarian cubicles far away in the bowels of the building. Now completely refurbished as a branch of the Dunfermline Building Society, it retains the look of an original. Next to Marlowe is a building which looks unwell. It has since been reconstructed and is now a B S M office. The man in the centre of the road is crossing towards the Playhouse. This, with its neighbour James Scott & Son Ltd, builders and fireplace specialists, at Nos 483–5, reveals the clearest evidence of domestic use of the upper storeys.*

The Playhouse's tale begins with the West End at No 475, a basic cinema dating from 1915 occupying an old billiard hall above the Aberdeen Dairy. The hall was leased from James Scott & Son, based next door, by James F Donald from Newhills. He had served an apprenticeship with John T Clark, coachbuilder and tramcar body builder across in Rose Street. He had spotted a likely venue for a new venture and from these humble beginnings grew the amazing Donald cinema and theatre dynasty. At the Ti'pinny Freezer – as the West End was nicknamed, owing to the dairy below – Donald kicked off with a single projector and a piano which accompanied not only the silent movies, but also the variety acts which were part of the show. The famous Willie Kemp came to sing cornkisters. James Donald's lease expired in 1920 and he was followed as tenant by Aberdeen Picture Palaces, which promptly closed the Freezer down for reconstruction. It reopened in 1921, splendidly refurbished, as the Playhouse.

Ushers in the Playhouse's distinctive foyer. *Bert Gates of Aberdeen Picture Palaces stands at the left. Young Nowheres? Surely not.*

In 1929, Aberdeen experienced the 'talkies' for the first time at the Playhouse, and the cinema continued in popularity until the days of decline. It closed in May 1974, to the regret of patrons. The lease was up, and James Scott & Son decided to dispose of their property. The two buildings were demolished to make way for Holburn House, an attractive, human-scale office development. West of the Playhouse and James Scott was a long, narrow shop at No 489, occupied by C H Webster, typewriter agent and cricketer. Aberdeen Photographic Services (always known as APS) was next door and Wishart the butcher was at No 493. In modern times, one of these small shops sold colourful Sicilian plates and dishes. Unfortunately it didn't survive.

Holburn Junction, looking east, 1956. *The last building on the south side (right) dates from the closing years of Union Place, as No 35. It has a slight nuance of Archibald Simpson. It was occupied by Chivas Bros from the 1880s, by Horne & Co., grocers, from around 1900 to 1910, and then by Chivas again until the Bank of Scotland arrived in the 1960s, eventually closing in August 2008 before vanishing completely the following month. St James Episcopal Church, by Arthur Clyne, 1887, keeks round the corner, right, but the street signage today indicates that it is neither in Union Street nor Holburn Street. Best seen from Alford Place, it patiently awaits its tower and spire. And can that be Madame Murray, extreme right?*

The North Side: From Summer Street to Alford Place

The north side of Union Place developed differently from the south. In *Aberdeen Awa'*, George Walker tells of John Cadenhead, a gardener who responded quickly to the idea. He feued out his market garden there, where tatties were his usual crop. According to Walker, 'his garden ground was feued, and the houses on it were originally built as summer residences for the citizens.' Substantial cottage-style houses rather than terraces of the south side were built in this section and are still found. We can go now to the starting point for the north side, the home stretch, the Summer Street junction.

Rather oddly, after the abolition of Union Place, the street numbers shoot upwards here, from No 262 at the NatWest Bank on the east side of Summer Street to No 402 at the Pizza Express on the west side. I don't think that Gilcomston South, on the corner, large and splendid kirk though it be, can have been allotted all these missing street numbers. The numbering on the south side is quite routine.

Gilcomston South Kirk, with its dramatic contrasting stonework and railings intact, around 1910. The kirk has skailed and folk are in Sunday best. Immediately right of the 'minaret', right, is a glimpse of a townhouse with a long ground-floor bay window. It is now part of the NatWest Bank, though the window has gone. Further right is the row of doctors' houses from Union Street West, not as yet broken up by the Amicable or the Majestic. Dr Angus Fraser's tall house is at the almost invisible Union Row junction, so the date must be a little before 1911. Left of the kirk, beyond the Summer Street junction, are the cottage-style buildings of the former Union Place.

The north side of Union Place starts with William 'Sweetie' Thomson's confectionery shop on the corner at Nos 402–8, visible in the picture opposite with two potential customers hovering outside. Thomson was there for more than half a century. Next door at No 412 (right of the carriage shop) and at a later date, was the excellent West End Bookshop which actively encouraged children to read and had a lending library downstairs. The 'West End' had acquired the business, including the steamer agency, from Alexander Murray, Madame's father. Murray had sought a haven on the north side when his original pitch was invaded by Milne's and Wyllie's. By the mid-1950s, the West End Bookshop became a branch of John Menzies, which is now owned by W H Smith.

The Gavin Bain Company property shop on the Chapel Street corner. *Latterly Fastframe, this was once Sim the Furrier, and just before the demise of the fur coat, the glamorous Jaffa Furs. Next door is the intriguingly named Falck Nutec Offshore Training Portal, almost overwhelmed by a mighty fascia, above which a spare fascia hovers. This little building once housed Adobe, which sold Mexican artefacts. Before that, there was a clothes shop, and one could go up its rickety stair to inspect rows of coloured shoes.*

Bryant Recruitment at No 440. *This is a handsome, timeless, late-nineteenth-century building, the first of four in this area, with interesting pilasters which shoot upwards in an attempt to become chimney pots.*

Two 'model houses'. *When this side of Union Place was being built up in the early nineteenth century, attention was drawn to two cottages, or 'model houses', on the east side of Rose Street. They are still here. (No sooner had they been photographed as Bean's than they became Caffè Nero). Archibald McKellar, family grocer, who not only sold pure malt whisky at three shillings a bottle, but also had an impressive range of 'medicinal wines', was an incumbent here. Later it became a branch of Burberry.*

Across the Rose Street divide, Fred Watt, gents' outfitter, was a fixture for many years, at No 464–6. In the mid-twentieth century one would also have found Ledinghams, the bakers, David Beck optician, W F Hay, chemist, The Divan at No 478, a tobacconist with Turkish connotations, rather than a furniture shop, A & J MacNab Drycleaners, and the former Waterhouse, already briefly encountered. No number was thought necessary, but it was beside No 40 Union Place. It later became Nos 478–84 Union Street, the second tall handsome building of the area, and as a 'Georgian', the oldest. The others are Victorian.

The Waterhouse – or Cistern, or Reservoir – came into being when water extraction from the Dee, essential for an expanding, thirsty city, was permitted by Parliament in 1829. The city architect, John Smith, was instructed to build a reservoir for its storage and distribution, hence the construction of the Waterhouse in 1830. Smith seems to have used his townhouse plans, as being most suitable for the locale. Inside the building were a vast lead-lined tank, machinery for distributing the water and a couple of offices. In 1866, the opening of the Invercanny waterworks rendered the Waterhouse redundant and it served as a fire station until 1872. It was then was acquired by the formidable William Bain for his carriage and horse hiring premises.

Union Place with a single tramline. The private house with steps, No 492, is next door to the Waterhouse, (opposite carriage), and the terrace, left again, is still intact at this point.

The Aberdeen Tramway Company has won the right to double the track and now, in the late nineteenth century, two tramlines are in evidence in Union Place. Next to the Waterhouse, left, the private house remains, but a tall handsome building, the third, Nos 496-500, has replaced the east half of the little terrace.

Bain's presence at the Waterhouse led to a cause célèbre in 1888. Aberdeen District Tramways, the horse tram company, had sought Parliamentary approval to double the tramway line in Union Street. Bain, who ran horse buses, petitioned the House of Commons against the doubling, which he saw as unfair competition. He argued that the road was too narrow and there was so much traffic at Holburn Junction that a double line would cause congestion and be dangerous. To reinforce his argument, he employed a photographer to take pictures of the junction of Holburn Street and Union Place crowded with vehicles. It was discovered that Bain was jam-packing the street outside his premises with his own vehicles, in particular 'a plumed hearse that occupied a conspicuous position in the throng of traffic'. Bain's subterfuge was revealed, his petition rejected and Union Street got its double tramline. Today there is a sizeable parking area behind the old Waterhouse, accessed from Thistle Place or a lane off Rose Street. This was once a busy area, the site of the Waterhouse workshops and Bain's stables and coach-houses. All gone.

By the early twentieth century, the Waterhouse was reconstructed and the upper floors became flats and office accommodation, while the British Linen Bank moved in on the ground floor. Half a century or so later, Chivas Bros, opposite at No 501, moved down to No 387 Union Street, to be replaced by the Bank of Scotland's West End branch. After the amalgamation of the two banks in 1971, No 501 became the chosen place of banking – though no longer. At the old Waterhouse, several other bank branches have since come and gone. Telephone and internet banking are taking their toll and the premises have been empty for some years. The firmly closed front doors of the old Waterhouse are in a sad state.

By the early twentieth century too, A & W Alexander, fish and game dealers, originally at No 476, had acquired the private house at No 492 and converted it into more convenient

*Left. **The Old Waterhouse**, glimpsed right, has become the British Linen Bank and the private house on its left at No 492 has lost its steps and railings and turned into A & W Alexander, fishmongers and game dealers, though the upper storeys remain the same. Alexander's window display always drew the crowds and used to be blamed for causing traffic accidents at Holburn Junction! Glimpsed left, Mitchell & Muil's jazzy new fascia contrasts with Alexander's sombre elegance. Right, a contemporary photograph of the former Waterhouse, deserted by its banking tenants. To the left is No 492, our private house with the steps which became A & W Alexander, then among others, Wm Low's supermarket of notorious memory, Joe Harper's Bar and now Beluga, 'the dining and drinking place'.*

premises. Here they remained until around 1963. They were succeeded by a branch of the Dundee supermarket chain, William Low & Co. This was historically interesting for it was an early move to self-service shopping. It was also the source of Aberdeen's infamous typhoid epidemic. In May 1964, slices from a six-pound can of Argentinian corned beef, infected with the typhoid organism, were sold from the cold counter. During the outbreak, over 500 people were taken ill. These were grim days, but the joke, of course, was that only 500 Aberdonians could share a six-pound can of corned beef. In fact the organism had spread to other parts of the shop. The city's state of siege was lifted on June 28 when the visit of the Queen to Aberdeen sounded the 'all clear'. William Low hung on another three years before closing. No 492 later became Joe Harper's Bar, run by the great man himself, and later still, Beluga – the drinking and dining place.

*Left. **Our third handsome building.** The central door is original and the window above retains its wrought iron 'balconette', one of several once in this area. Endsleigh Insurance, No 500, left, departed in August 2008 but Mitchell & Muil's closed shop, No 496, has been transformed into a Starbucks, with a simple elegant frontage, right.*

At Holburn Junction, Union Street takes on a different aspect as it makes the gentle curve into Alford Place. MacKeggie, the newsagent, was at No 516 from the early days – indeed the original G L MacKeggie had taken over from a Union Place newsagent. As well as running an above average newsagency, MacKeggie at one time offered printing services, made rubber stamps, and acted as a stationer, selling exercise books, pencils and rulers to schoolchildren. In the old days, there were as many shops in Union Street serving the academic needs of schoolchildren as there are currently attending to their gastronomic requirements. R S McColl took over when MacKeggie closed, but it wasn't the same.

The north side of Union Street vanishes round the corner to end at No 520. At the left of this picture is the fourth high and handsome building, where Nan K Johnson sold elegant furs and astrakhan coats for what seemed like a lifetime. The fast food shops here now display conflicting garish green fascias. FoneXtra, centre, was once a gift shop. MacKeggie's was to its left. The surviving half of the original little terrace is to its right.

Journey's end: Holburn Junction, 1947. *We can bid farewell to Union Street at Holburn Junction, looking towards Holburn Street, left, and Alford Place right. A man in a suit and a lady in a hat wander across the middle of the road in the sunlight and a No 3 Queen's Cross tram is about to take on passengers at Christ's College. Its narrow route band, a distinctive pale orange, is below the upper windows. Happy days!*

GLOSSARY

Aberdeen on a Flag Day: famous Aberdeen postcard joke showing an empty Union Street while thrifty Aberdonians stay at home to avoid having to buy a flag. The reverse is *Aberdeen on a House-to-House Collection Day* when Union Street is crammed with people.

advocate (in Aberdeen): a solicitor.

ashlar: squares of finely cut masonry.

balconette: a cast-iron window box or diminutive balcony.

campanile: a slender bell tower, used here as a comparison.

The Disruption: In 1843, after years of conflict over (among other things) a congregation's right to choose its minister, 450 ministers of the Church of Scotland broke away to form the Free Church of Scotland. The Free Kirk and the Established Church were reunited in 1929. Aberdeen was a Free Kirk stronghold, which is one reason for the large number of redundant churches in the city.

fenestration: the arrangement of windows in a building.

feu: a former type of landholding, by which land, houses, etc. were held in perpetuity on payment of an annual sum of money called feu duty.

finial: an ornament, such as a ball or an animal, at the top of a spire, gable, gatepost, etc.

Gibbs surround: A door or window surround with alternating large and small blocks of stone. Used by the Aberdeen architect, James Gibbs.

Ionic: a style of pillar with spiral scrolls (volutes), like stylised curling rams' horns, decorating its capital. See Music Hall pillars, page 133.

List: A list of Buildings of Architectural or Historical Interest (usually A or B, according to merit) originally compiled on behalf of the Secretary of State for Scotland.

oriel: a bay window supported on brackets.

pediment: a triangular gable.

pilaster: a shallow, square column , usually 'engaged' i.e. partially built into the wall.

portico: an outsize porch.

rusticated: blocks of masonry emphasised by deeply recessed joints. See page 53, top.

INDEX